The Ultimate

Interview

Preparation Guide

Author

Diksha Arora

Published By

Invincible Publication Pvt. Ltd.

Published by:
Invincible Publication Pvt.Ltd.
1103-A, 11th Floor SAS Tower, Sector 38,
Gurugram, Haryana – 122003
Email: sales@i-publish.in
Website : www.invinciblepublishers.com

Sales Office : - 4760-61/23, Basement, Pratap Street, Ansari Road,
Daryaganj, New Delhi - 110002
Email: invinciblepublishers@gmail.com

ISBN : 978-93-5886-817-3

Book Name : The Ultimate Interview Preparation Guide
Author: Diksha Arora
First Edition: 2025

The Ultimate Interview Preparation Guide

Diksha Arora

PREFACE

Interviews are often seen as daunting experiences, yet they represent transformative moments that can shape the trajectory of one's career. Through my journey as an interview coach, I've had the privilege of working with thousands of candidates—freshers and experienced professionals alike—helping them overcome their fears, sharpen their skills, and secure opportunities with some of the world's top companies. "***The Ultimate Interview Preparation Guide***" is a culmination of those experiences, designed to empower readers with the tools they need to excel at every stage of the interview process.

This book goes beyond just preparing for interview questions. It offers a holistic approach to landing your dream job, covering key topics such as crafting ***ATS-friendly resumes*** that get noticed, mastering the art of ***salary negotiation,*** and applying proven ***interview techniques*** that leave a lasting impression. Additionally, I've included ***250+ sample answers*** to the toughest interview questions faced by both freshers and seasoned professionals. These answers are designed to inspire confidence and help you tailor your responses to reflect your unique strengths.

What makes this guide special is its practical, step-by-step approach, informed by real-world insights from my work with candidates across various industries. It's a resource for anyone seeking not just to survive the interview process but to thrive in it. Whether you're re-entering the workforce, transitioning into a new field, or preparing for your very first interview, this book is here to guide you every step of the way.

Every page of this book "***The Ultimate Interview Preparation Guide***" reflects my passion for helping individuals achieve their career aspirations and my firm belief that preparation is the foundation of success. Interviews are not just about answering questions—they're about telling your story with clarity, confidence, and authenticity.

As you embark on your journey, remember:

"Success is where preparation and opportunity meet." – Bobby Unser

Wishing you the best in achieving your dreams,

Diksha Arora | Interview Coach

ACKNOWLEDGMENT

Writing "***The Ultimate Interview Preparation Guide***" has been an incredible journey, and I would not have been able to achieve this milestone without the unwavering support of the people who mean the most to me.

First and foremost, I want to express my deepest gratitude to my parents, ***Dr. Roma Manglani*** and ***Sanjay Manglani***, for their unconditional love, encouragement, and belief in me. Mom, your wisdom and strength have always inspired me to aim higher, and Dad, your constant support has given me the confidence to pursue my dreams. Thank you both for being my pillars of strength and guiding lights in every step of my life.

A big thank you to the ***Invincible team***, my publishers, for their incredible dedication and expertise in bringing this book to life. Your meticulous efforts have ensured that this book reaches its fullest potential, and I am truly grateful for your partnership.

To my amazing candidates: this book is for you. Your hard work, perseverance, and success stories have been my greatest motivation. Each result you've achieved has been a testament to what we can accomplish together, and I am endlessly inspired by your determination to excel. Thank you for trusting me to be a part of your journey.

This book is a labor of love, fueled by the belief that every candidate has the potential to succeed. I hope it serves as a valuable resource to help many more achieve their dreams.

With gratitude

Diksha Arora | Interview Coach

INDEX

- 4.6.3. Are you applying to other companies as well?
- 4.6.4. Why do you want this job?
- 4.6.5. Why are you interviewing for this company when you already have a job offer?
- 4.6.6. What are your future plans?

4.7 Section 7: Leadership Skills

- 4.7.1. Describe a time when you had to take charge of a situation?
- 4.7.2. How do you handle tough decisions?
- 4.7.3. What strategies do you use to motivate your team?
- 4.7.4. What have been your most successful leadership experiences and why?
- 4.7.5. How do you ensure everyone on the team is working towards the same goal?
- 4.7.6. What do you think are the most important qualities of an effective leader?

4.8 Section 8: General

- 4.8.1. Do you like to work alone or with a team?
- 4.8.2. What motivates you?
- 4.8.3. Are you willing to work overtime?
- 4.8.4. Are you applying to other companies as well?
- 4.8.5. What was the most difficult decision you made?
- 4.8.6. Tell me about something that is not mentioned on your resume
- 4.8.7. Do you consider yourself successful?
- 4.8.8. Do you have any plans for further education?
- 4.8.9. What is the most important aspect for you in your job?

CHAPTER 1

PREPARING FOR PRE-SCREENING PHONE CALLS

1.1 What are pre-screening phone calls?

After submitting the resumes, candidates often start receiving interview calls. However, many fail to recognize the significance of these pre-screening phone calls. How you handle these initial conversations can directly impact whether you're shortlisted for a formal interview or not.

Pre-screening phone calls serve as the first stage of the interview process. Typically conducted by recruiters or hiring managers, these calls aim to evaluate a candidate's basic qualifications and suitability for the role before proceeding further. They usually last between **10 to 30 minutes** and focus on critical aspects such as:

Resume Review:	Skills and Expectations:	Logistical Details:
Confirming your qualifications and work experience.	Discussing your core competencies, career goals, and job expectations.	Clarifying your availability, notice period, and salary expectations.

These calls are essential for employers to filter candidates who align with the job requirements, streamlining the hiring process.

Candidates who handle these calls professionally and communicate effectively are often informed about the next steps in the process, such as scheduling formal interviews. Treat these calls as a vital opportunity to make a positive first impression and position yourself as a strong contender for the role.

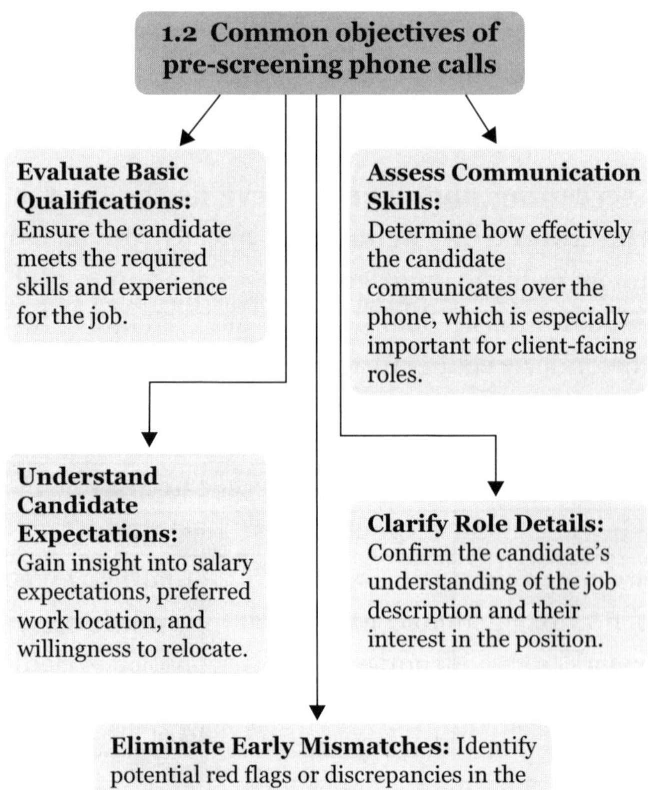

1.3 How to prepare for pre-screening phone calls?

Preparation is key to making a strong first impression during a pre-screening phone call. Follow these steps:

1. **Review the Job Description:** Understand the role, required qualifications, and key responsibilities. This helps you align your answers with what the employer is looking for.
2. **Update Your Resume:** Ensure your resume is accurate and highlights your most relevant experiences and achievements. Be ready to discuss any gaps or transitions in your career.
3. **Research the Company:** Familiarize yourself with the company's mission, values, and recent developments to demonstrate genuine interest.
4. **Prepare Common Answers:** Practice answering 'frequently asked pre-screening questions', such as:
   - Tell me about yourself.
   - What are the recent projects that you have worked on?
   - Why are you interested in this position?
   - Why are you leaving your previous job?
   - Are you willing to relocate?
   - What is your current salary and notice period?

Q. Tell me about yourself

Hints to answer:

- Start with your current role, mentioning your job title and key responsibilities.
- Highlight a significant achievement or skill relevant to the position.
- Conclude with a brief mention of your future goals aligning with the role you're applying for.

Q. What are the recent projects that you have worked on?

Hints to answer:

- Briefly describe the project's objective and your role in it.
- Highlight the skills and tools you used.
- Share the impact or outcome of the project, focusing on measurable results.

Q. Why are you interested in this position?

Hints to answer:

- Discuss how the role aligns with your career goals.
- Mention what excites you about the company or its values.
- Highlight how your skills and experience make you a strong fit for the role.

SAMPLE RESPONSE: I'm excited about this role because it aligns perfectly with my skills in [mention relevant skills] and offers an opportunity to contribute to [company's goals or projects].

Q. Why are you leaving your previous job?

Hints to answer:

- Focus on positive reasons like career growth, seeking new challenges, or aligning with long-term goals.
- Avoid negative comments about your current employer.
- Emphasize how this role provides a better opportunity to achieve your aspirations.

SAMPLE RESPONSE: I'm looking for new challenges and career growth opportunities that this role can provide, which align better with my long-term professional goals.

Q. Are you willing to relocate?

Hints to answer:

- Answer honestly based on your situation.
- If yes, express enthusiasm about exploring new opportunities.
- If no, briefly explain constraints but express openness to remote options if available.

Q. What is your current salary and notice period?

Hints to answer:

- Provide an honest and concise response.
- Mention your current salary and add, "I'm open to discussing a competitive compensation package based on the role and responsibilities."
- State your notice period, emphasizing your readiness to join as soon as possible.

Current CTC (Sample Answer)

"My current CTC is [insert amount], and I'm looking for a competitive package that reflects the responsibilities of this role."

Notice Period (Different Situations)

- **Standard Situation:**

SAMPLE RESPONSE: My notice period is [insert number of weeks/months], and I can join as soon as this period is completed.

- **Immediate Availability:**

SAMPLE RESPONSE: I can join immediately as I'm in a position to transition quickly.

- **Longer Notice Period:**

SAMPLE RESPONSE: My current notice period is [insert number of weeks/months], but I am open to negotiating an earlier start date if necessary.

5. **Set Up Your Environment:** Choose a quiet location with no distractions, and ensure a good phone connection.
6. **Keep Notes Handy:** Keep your resume, the job description, and a list of key achievements or important points you want to mention close by for quick reference. However, avoid relying on your notes too much—it should never appear as if you're reading from them.

PRO TIP: Start preparing for interviews the moment you begin circulating your resume. Don't wait for the interview to be scheduled to start your prep. Confidently answering pre-screening calls is a critical step in moving closer to securing your dream job!

1.4 Do's and don'ts during a pre-screening phone call

Do's:	Don'ts:
Answer Promptly: Pick up the call on time and greet the recruiter politely.	**Don't Sound Distracted:** Avoid multitasking during the call or speaking in a noisy environment.
Speak Clearly: Use a confident tone and articulate your thoughts concisely.	**Don't Provide Excessive Details:** Keep your responses focused and relevant.
Be Honest: Provide accurate information about your qualifications, skills, and availability.	**Don't Mention Salary First:** Let the recruiter bring up the topic unless explicitly asked.
Ask Questions: Inquire about the role, team structure, or next steps in the hiring process if given the opportunity.	**Don't Oversell Yourself:** Be genuine and don't exaggerate your qualifications or experience.

CHAPTER 2

INTERVIEW PREPARATION TIPS THAT YOU CAN'T MISS

2.1 Company Research

Before stepping into an interview, one of the most important things you can do is research the company thoroughly. **Understand its mission, vision, culture, products or services, and recent developments.** Knowing the company will not only help you tailor your responses to fit their values but also help you ask intelligent questions, showing your genuine interest.

Key Points to Research:

1.	**Company's history and background:**	Understand when and how the company was founded, its journey, and its key milestones in becoming an industry leader. You can easily find all this information on the company's website.
2.	**Products, services, and recent news:**	Familiarize yourself with the company's offerings and any recent product launches or news that highlight its innovation and market position.

3.	**Company values and culture:**	Research the company's core values and workplace culture to understand what they prioritize, such as teamwork, innovation, or customer-centricity.
4.	**Competitors in the market:**	Identify the company's key competitors and what differentiates the company from them in terms of offerings or market strategy.
5.	**Achievements and any major challenges the company is facing:**	Highlight the company's recent successes, like awards or market share growth, and recognize any current challenges it is addressing in the industry.
6.	**Financial health:**	Assess the company's financial stability by looking at its revenue trends, profitability, debt levels, and market performance to understand its ability to sustain growth and weather economic fluctuations.

Sources to Research About the Company:

1. **Company's Website:** The company's official website is the most reliable source for detailed information about its history, mission, products, services, values, and leadership.

2. **Google News:** Search for the company's name on Google News to find recent articles, press releases, or updates that could provide insights into new developments or challenges the company is facing.
3. **Social Media Handles:**

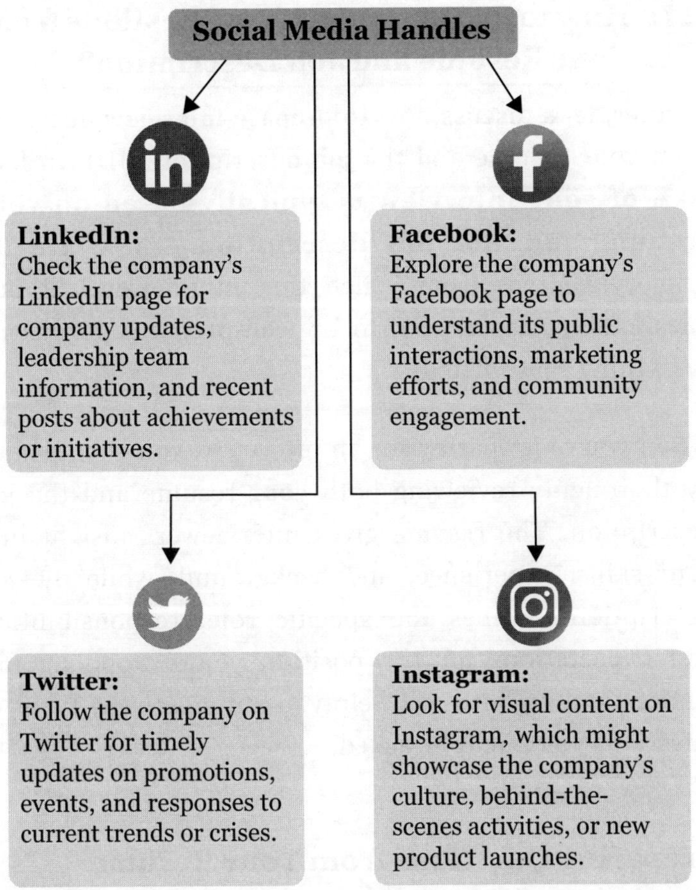

4. **Glassdoor or Indeed:** Explore employee reviews and ratings to understand the company culture, work environment, and common employee sentiments.

5. **Annual Reports and Financial Statements:** For publicly traded companies, these documents are often available on their website or through financial platforms like Yahoo Finance or Bloomberg, offering insights into financial health and key achievements.

2.2 How to Prepare Interview Questions from Your Resume and Job Description?

Further, let's discuss how to prepare interview questions from your resume and the job description (JD). In fact, **70% of your interview is typically based on your resume and the job description**. These are the primary sources from which the interviewer will pull questions, so it's crucial to be well-prepared to discuss everything that's listed.

When you're preparing for an interview, you should start by thoroughly reviewing both your resume and the job description. The resume gives interviewers insight into your skills, experience, and background, while the job description outlines the specific role, responsibilities, and expectations for the position you're applying for. Understanding both will help you anticipate the types of questions you might be asked.

Preparing Questions from Your Resume

Let's understand this with the help of a sample resume:-

Aditi Khanna

Feature Writer

aditixxxx@gmail.com | +91-xxxxxxxxxx | [LinkedIn URL]

Q1. Tell us something about yourself

Profile Summary

Dynamic, detail-oriented, and results-driven journalist with X years of experience in writing and editing for both digital and print media. Adept at creating engaging content that resonates with diverse audiences while adhering to editorial standards. Known for my entrepreneurial spirit, strong networking skills, and the ability to manage and deliver high-quality work under tight deadlines.

Q2. Can you tell us about your experience as a feature writer in HT Labs?

Professional Experience

Feature Writer

HT Labs, New Delhi

January 2022 – Present

- Wrote and published over 100 feature articles and explainers on current affairs and evergreen topics, increasing readership by 30% through targeted content.
- Applied comprehensive knowledge of public opinion, social media trends, and traditional media

to craft attention-grabbing stories, resulting in a 25% increase in social media engagement.

- Developed marketing content such as blogs, promotional materials, and copy for social media, contributing to a 20% growth in the company's online visibility.
- Collaborated with cross-functional teams to ensure seamless integration of editorial and marketing efforts, enhancing the overall brand presence.

Q3. Can you walk us through a specific article you wrote that had a significant impact?

Q4. What strategies did you use to increase the SME by 25%?

Assistant Manager (Content)

Info Edge, Noida

December 2020 – January 2022

- Created and updated education-related wiki pages for 50+ universities and colleges, significantly improving content accuracy and engagement on the platform.
- Managed and tracked real-time education news and alerts, ensuring timely publication of relevant content and updates.
- Worked closely with the **SEO team, helping drive a 15% increase in organic search traffic** to the company's education pages.

Q5. What was your role at SEO efforts an Info edge? How did you help drive 15% increase in organic traffic?

Social Media-cum-Outreach Manager

Global Classroom, Lucknow

March 2017 – July 2017

- Created and managed content for company products and services, resulting **in a 40% increase in engagement** across social media channels.
- Led social media campaigns that **increased brand awareness** and customer interaction, improving customer inquiries by 20%.

Q6. How do you ensure content remains engaging? Can you give examples

Q7. What tools do you use to increase brand awareness?

Skills

- Networking and Relationship Building
- Feature Writing & Journalism
- Editorial Functions & Content Management
- Social Media Strategy and Outreach
- Data-Driven Storytelling

Skill-Related Questions

How do you leverage your networking skills?

How do you approach relationship building with your audience?

What are the most critical aspects of feature writing?

Tools that you use to track & measure the success of your content

Example of how you have used data in your stories

Certifications

- Digital Marketing Fundamentals (Google Digital Garage, 2024)
- Content Marketing (HubSpot Academy, 2023)
- SEO Fundamentals (SEMrush Academy, 2023)

Education

2019 — UGC-NET (Journalism and Mass Communication)

2015 — M.A. in Journalism and Mass Communication, Amity University, Noida

Certification and Education-Related Questions:

1. How have your certifications in Digital Marketing, Content Marketing, and SEO helped you in your content development roles?

2. How does your education in Journalism and Mass Communication influence your writing and content strategies?
3. Can you share how your UGC-NET qualification has contributed to your expertise in journalism and writing?

Other questions that can be asked are:-

Problem-Solving and Impact-Related Questions:

1. Describe a time when you had to create content on a tight deadline. How did you manage to produce high-quality work?
2. Can you provide an example where your content directly influenced audience engagement or customer interaction?
3. Have you ever faced challenges while working on a feature article? How did you overcome them?

Future-Forward Questions:

1. Where do you see yourself in the next 2–3 years in terms of career development within journalism?
2. What kinds of content or writing projects are you most passionate about, and why?
3. How do you stay updated with trends in journalism and content creation?

Conclusion

In conclusion, as you prepare for your interviews, it is essential to anticipate and prepare for questions derived from your resume. Interviewers may focus on the following key aspects:

1. Personality-Related Questions
2. Projects You Have Worked On
3. Your Achievements
4. Skill-Related Questions
5. Problem-Solving and Confidence Testing
6. Career Transitions or Gaps
7. Teamwork and Collaboration
8. Leadership and Initiative
9. Adaptability and Learning
10. Future Goals and Aspirations
11. Industry Knowledge and Passion

NOTE: We will be covering all the important interview questions related to each aspect in detail further in the book.

2.3 How to prepare interview questions from the job description?

Understanding a job description (JD) is one of the most crucial steps in preparing for an interview. A JD provides insights into the expectations of the role, the skills required, and the key responsibilities. To ace an interview, candidates should analyze the JD thoroughly to anticipate the types of questions that may be asked. This chapter will guide you through the process of preparing interview questions using a real-life JD as an example.

We'll take the example of a **Design Consultant - Senior Analyst** position at Deloitte and break down the steps to formulate questions based on the JD provided.

Step 1: Analyze the Job Description

Begin by breaking down the JD into the following categories:

1.	Key Skills and Experience	What specific skills are required?
2.	Responsibilities	What tasks will you perform on the job?
3.	Tools and Software	What technical expertise is mentioned?
4.	Soft Skills	What personal attributes or communication skills are emphasized?

SAMPLE JD

Design Consultant - Senior Analyst

Deloitte · Hyderabad, Telangana, India

Key Skills And Experience Required

- Should have worked in an eLearning firm
- Proficient with MS Office (MS Word and PowerPoint)
- Demonstrate knowledge of courseware development tools such as Articulate Storyline, Adobe Captivate, Articulate Presenter, and Lectora
- Demonstrate excellent writing and project management skills
- Demonstrate strong communication skills and the ability to interact at all levels
- Understand learning needs and project specifications
- Ability to write crisp and effective instruction
- Created and revised storyboards for various delivery formats—ILT/CBT/WBT
- Worked with graphic designers and programmers in developing the end product within given timelines

Step 2: Formulate Questions from each section of the JD

Here's how to prepare potential interview questions from each section:

Question 1: Can you share your experience working in an eLearning firm and the type of projects you handled?

Purpose: To validate your industry experience.

Question 2: Can you describe how you've used MS Word and PowerPoint in previous roles, particularly for courseware development?"

Purpose: To assess your technical proficiency.

Question 3: Which courseware development tools are you most comfortable with, and can you share an example of a project where you used them effectively?

Purpose: To gauge your hands-on experience with specific tools.

Question 4: How have you used your communication skills to collaborate with team members or stakeholders at different levels?

Purpose: To understand your ability to work across hierarchies.

Question 5: Can you give an example of a project you managed from start to finish? How did you ensure timely delivery and quality?

Purpose: To assess your organizational and leadership skills.

Question 6: What approach do you take when creating or revising storyboards for different delivery formats like ILT, CBT, or WBT?"

Purpose: To evaluate your understanding of instructional design principles.

Question 7: Can you share an instance where you collaborated with designers and programmers to meet a tight deadline? How did you handle challenges?

Purpose: To explore your teamwork and problem-solving abilities.

Final Step: **Broaden the Scope**

After preparing JD-specific questions, anticipate related topics:

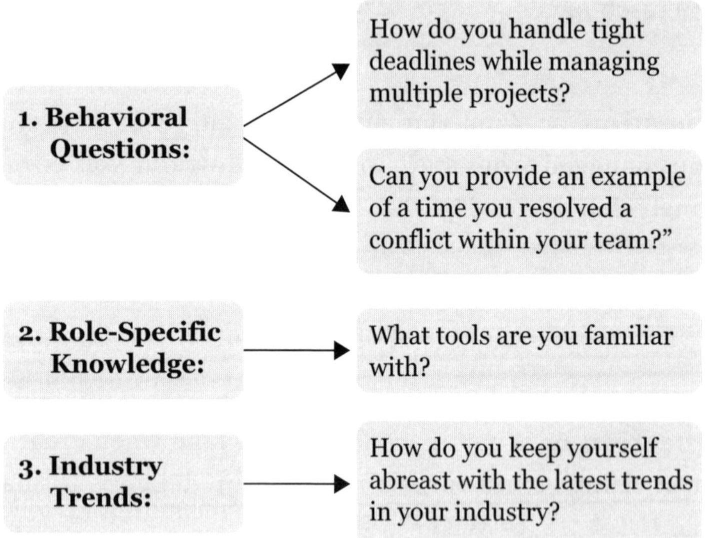

Conclusion

When preparing questions from a JD:

1.	**Understand the role requirements**	Study the JD line by line to identify the key skills, tools, and responsibilities.
2.	**Match your experience**	Frame questions that help you highlight your relevant achievements and expertise.
3.	**Prepare for behavioral and situational questions**	Use examples from your past to answer questions effectively.
4.	**Research the company**	Learn about the organization's culture, projects, and goals to align your responses with their expectations.
5.	**Practice your answers**	Use mock interviews or record yourself to ensure your responses are clear and confident.

Pro Tip: Preparing for interview questions based on your resume and the job description is key to a successful interview. Make sure to align your experiences, skills, and qualifications, and be ready to discuss how you can add value to the company. By taking time to review these two documents carefully, you will feel more confident and ready to handle 70% of the questions that come your way during the interview.

2.4 Understanding the Interview Format

Understanding the interview format can help you prepare in a way that's tailored to the specific structure of the interview.

Here are different type of interview formats:-

Technical or HR Interviews:

Know whether the interview will be more focused on assessing your technical abilities (coding, problem-solving, etc.) or your interpersonal and behavioral skills.

Case Study or Problem Solving:

Some interviews may include practical tests or case study questions, especially in fields like software engineering, business consulting, or data analysis.

Panel Interview:

If you are facing a panel of interviewers, it's crucial to maintain eye contact with all members and engage with everyone.

Virtual Interviews:

With the rise of remote interviews, it's important to prepare for a smooth virtual experience—test your equipment, ensure good lighting, and focus on clear communication.

Knowing the format helps you manage expectations and avoid surprises, ensuring you perform your best during the interview.

2.5 What to say – When you don't know the answer to an interview question

Sometimes in an interview, you might encounter a question you're unprepared for. The way you respond in such moments reflects your composure, problem-solving ability, and willingness to learn. Here's how to handle these situations gracefully, along with phrases you can use depending on the specific scenario:

1. When You Need Clarification on the Question

If the question seems unclear or too broad, ask for clarification. This shows that you're thoughtful and want to provide a precise answer.

- **Phrases to Use:**
  - "Could you please clarify what you mean by [specific term]?"
  - "I'd like to ensure I'm addressing the question correctly. Are you asking about [restate your understanding]?"
  - "Can you provide an example to help me better understand the context?"

2. When You Don't Have Immediate Knowledge

If you're unsure of the answer but can figure it out with time or resources, demonstrate your willingness to learn and problem-solve.

- **Phrases to Use:**
  - "That's a great question. I don't have the answer at the moment, but I'd be happy to research and follow up with you."
  - "I haven't encountered this situation before, but I'm confident I could figure it out by [explaining your approach]."
  - "I'm not entirely sure, but here's how I would approach solving this problem."

3. When You're Unfamiliar with a Concept

If the question pertains to a concept or skill you don't know, emphasize your adaptability and willingness to learn.

- **Phrases to Use:**
  - "I haven't worked with [specific tool/concept] directly, but I'm eager to learn and have successfully picked up similar skills like [related example]."
  - "While I'm not familiar with [specific term], I have experience with [related area] and am confident I can bridge the gap quickly."
  - "I appreciate the opportunity to learn about this area—it's something I'm keen to explore further."

4. When the Question Is Unexpected or Unconventional

For tricky or unexpected questions, take a moment to think, and then provide a thoughtful response—even if it's not perfect.

- **Phrases to Use:**
  - "That's an interesting question. Let me take a moment to think about it."
  - "I haven't considered that perspective before, but here's how I might approach it."
  - "This is a new angle for me. My initial thought is [share your reasoning], but I'd love to explore it further."

5. When You've Forgotten Something Relevant

If you know the answer but can't recall it at the moment, acknowledge it honestly and explain how you would find the information.

- **Phrases to Use:**
  - "I've worked with this concept before, but I can't recall the specifics right now. I would approach it by [explain your problem-solving method]."
  - "I'm drawing a blank at the moment, but I know where to look for the answer or how to approach it."
  - "I've encountered this before, and while I can't recall the exact details, I'd revisit [specific resource] to confirm."

6. When You Don't Know and Can't Speculate

If the question is entirely out of your expertise, it's best to be honest while showing curiosity and a proactive attitude.

- **Phrases to Use:**
  - "I'm not familiar with this topic, but I'd love to learn more about it. Could you provide additional context?"
  - "This isn't an area I've worked on before, but I'm very interested in expanding my knowledge here."
  - "I don't have experience in this domain yet, but I'm open to learning and would love to explore this further if given the opportunity."

Bonus Tips:

1. **Stay Calm and Composed:** It's okay not to know everything. How you handle the situation matters more than having the perfect answer.
2. **Buy Yourself Time:** If you need a moment to think, use phrases like:
   - "Let me take a moment to think about that."
   - "That's an excellent question. Let me gather my thoughts."
3. **Circle Back if Possible:** If you remember the answer later in the interview, mention it confidently:
   - "Earlier, we discussed [question], and I wanted to revisit it. Here's how I'd approach it."

Conclusion:

Not knowing an answer isn't a deal-breaker—it's an opportunity to showcase your honesty, adaptability, and problem-solving approach. By using these phrases, you can handle such situations with professionalism and confidence.

NOTES

CHAPTER 3

HOW TO WRITE AN ATS-FRIENDLY RESUME?

In today's competitive job market, your resume isn't just reviewed by hiring managers; it's also screened by Applicant Tracking Systems (ATS). This chapter will guide you through crafting a resume that not only highlights your qualifications but also successfully passes through ATS filters.

3.1 What is an ATS?

Applicant Tracking Systems (ATS) are software programs used by companies to streamline the hiring process. They help filter, rank, and sort resumes based on keywords and predefined criteria, making it easier for recruiters to find the best candidates.

While ATS simplifies the recruitment process for employers, it adds a layer of complexity for job seekers. **If your resume isn't optimized for ATS, it might never reach the hands of a recruiter, no matter how qualified you are.**

3.2 Tips for Creating an ATS-Friendly Resume

1.	**Use Standard Formatting:**	Avoid using elaborate templates or graphics. Stick to a clean, simple format with standard fonts like Arial, Times New Roman, or Calibri.
2.	**Include Relevant Keywords:**	Tailor your resume for each job application. Use keywords directly from the job description that align with your skills and experience.
3.	**Use Standard Headings:**	Stick to conventional headings like "Work Experience," "Education," "Skills," etc. ATS may not recognize creative headings.
4.	**Avoid Tables and Columns:**	Most ATS struggle to read information presented in tables or multiple columns. Use simple bullet points instead.
5.	**Save in the Right Format:**	Save your resume as a .docx or .pdf file. However, check the job posting to ensure compatibility.
6.	**Avoid Special Characters:**	Steer clear of special characters, graphics, and images. They can confuse the ATS.

7.	**Spell Out Abbreviations:**	If you use acronyms, ensure you spell them out at least once (e.g., "Customer Relationship Management (CRM)").
8.	**Proofread for Errors:**	Even a small typo can make your resume appear unprofessional and might result in rejection.

3.3 Ideal Resume Format

1. Header

- Include your full name, phone number, email address, and LinkedIn profile URL. Ensure your email is professional and avoid using your current work email.

2. Professional Summary

- Write a concise 2-3 sentence summary highlighting your key skills and accomplishments. Tailor it for each job application.

3. Skills

- List relevant skills in a bullet-point format. Use both technical and soft skills as mentioned in the job description. Keep changing this section as per the job description.

4. Work Experience

- Use reverse-chronological order (most recent first).
- Include the job title, company name, location, and employment dates.
- Use bullet points to describe your responsibilities and achievements, incorporating relevant keywords.

5. Education

- Mention your degree, institution, location, and graduation year.
- Include certifications if relevant.

6. Additional Sections

- **Certifications:** List industry-relevant certifications.
- **Volunteer Work:** Include only if it's significant and relevant.
- **Projects:** Highlight key projects showcasing your skills.

Sample Resume Template For Freshers

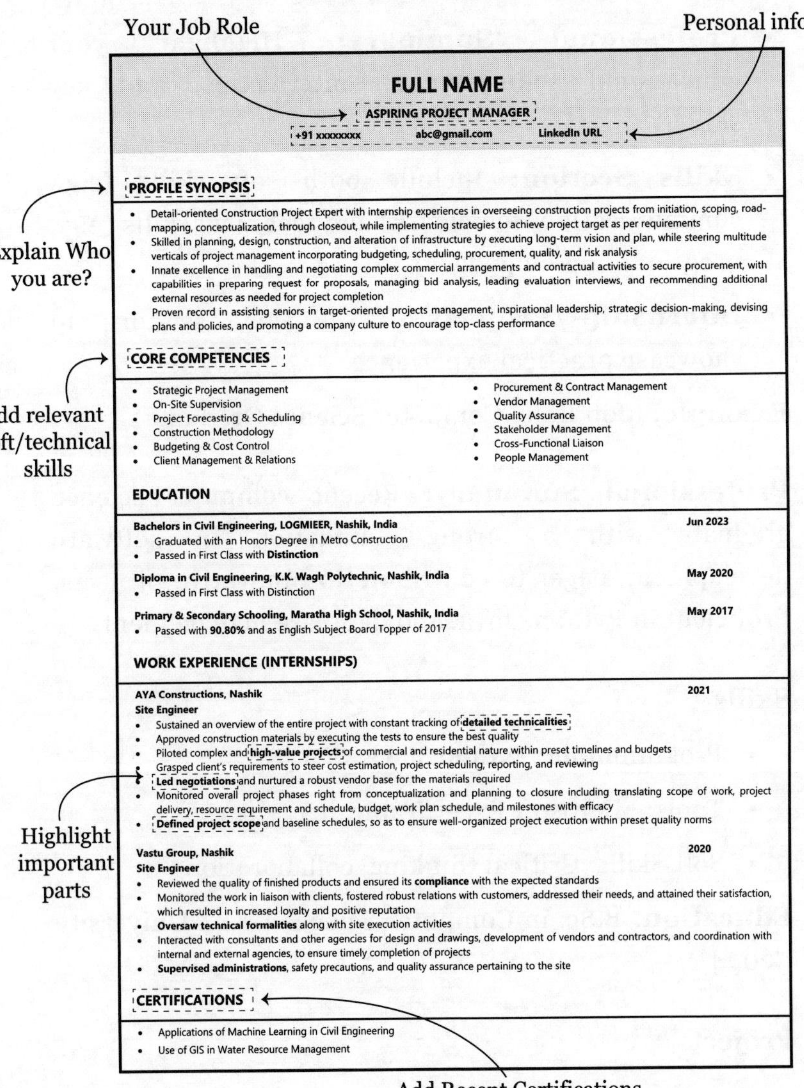

FULL NAME

ASPIRING PROJECT MANAGER

+91 xxxxxxxx **abc@gmail.com** **LinkedIn URL**

PROFILE SYNOPSIS

- Detail-oriented Construction Project Expert with internship experiences in overseeing construction projects from initiation, scoping, road-mapping, conceptualization, through closeout, while implementing strategies to achieve project target as per requirements
- Skilled in planning, design, construction, and alteration of infrastructure by executing long-term vision and plan, while steering multitude verticals of project management incorporating budgeting, scheduling, procurement, quality, and risk analysis
- Innate excellence in handling and negotiating complex commercial arrangements and contractual activities to secure procurement, with capabilities in preparing request for proposals, managing bid analysis, leading evaluation interviews, and recommending additional external resources as needed for project completion
- Proven record in assisting seniors in target-oriented projects management, inspirational leadership, strategic decision-making, devising plans and policies, and promoting a company culture to encourage top-class performance

CORE COMPETENCIES

- Strategic Project Management
- On-Site Supervision
- Project Forecasting & Scheduling
- Construction Methodology
- Budgeting & Cost Control
- Client Management & Relations
- Procurement & Contract Management
- Vendor Management
- Quality Assurance
- Stakeholder Management
- Cross-Functional Liaison
- People Management

EDUCATION

Bachelors in Civil Engineering, LOGMIEER, Nashik, India **Jun 2023**
- Graduated with an Honors Degree in Metro Construction
- Passed in First Class with **Distinction**

Diploma in Civil Engineering, K.K. Wagh Polytechnic, Nashik, India **May 2020**
- Passed in First Class with Distinction

Primary & Secondary Schooling, Maratha High School, Nashik, India **May 2017**
- Passed with **90.80%** and as English Subject Board Topper of 2017

WORK EXPERIENCE (INTERNSHIPS)

AYA Constructions, Nashik **2021**
Site Engineer
- Sustained an overview of the entire project with constant tracking of **detailed technicalities**
- Approved construction materials by executing the tests to ensure the best quality
- Piloted complex and **high-value projects** of commercial and residential nature within preset timelines and budgets
- Grasped client's requirements to steer cost estimation, project scheduling, reporting, and reviewing
- **Led negotiations** and nurtured a robust vendor base for the materials required
- Monitored overall project phases right from conceptualization and planning to closure including translating scope of work, project delivery, resource requirement and schedule, budget, work plan schedule, and milestones with efficacy
- **Defined project scope** and baseline schedules, so as to ensure well-organized project execution within preset quality norms

Vastu Group, Nashik **2020**
Site Engineer
- Reviewed the quality of finished products and ensured its **compliance** with the expected standards
- Monitored the work in liaison with clients, fostered robust relations with customers, addressed their needs, and attained their satisfaction, which resulted in increased loyalty and positive reputation
- **Oversaw technical formalities** along with site execution activities
- Interacted with consultants and other agencies for design and drawings, development of vendors and contractors, and coordination with internal and external agencies, to ensure timely completion of projects
- **Supervised administrations**, safety precautions, and quality assurance pertaining to the site

CERTIFICATIONS

- Applications of Machine Learning in Civil Engineering
- Use of GIS in Water Resource Management

3.4 Resume Tips for Freshers

Focus Areas

- **Professional Summary:** Highlight your educational achievements, internships, and key skills.
- **Skills Section:** Include both soft skills (e.g., communication, teamwork) and technical skills (e.g., programming languages).
- **Internships/Projects:** Use this section to showcase practical experience.

Example: (Job Role: Computer Science Graduate)

Professional Summary: Recent computer science graduate with a strong foundation in software development, eager to contribute to innovative projects. Proficient in Python, Java, and database management.

Skills

- Programming: Python, Java, SQL
- Tools: Microsoft Excel, Tableau
- Soft Skills: Critical thinking, collaboration

Education: B.Sc. in Computer Science | XYZ University | 2024

Projects

- **E-commerce Website:** Developed a fully functional e-commerce platform using Python and Django.

Sample Resume Template For Experienced Professionals

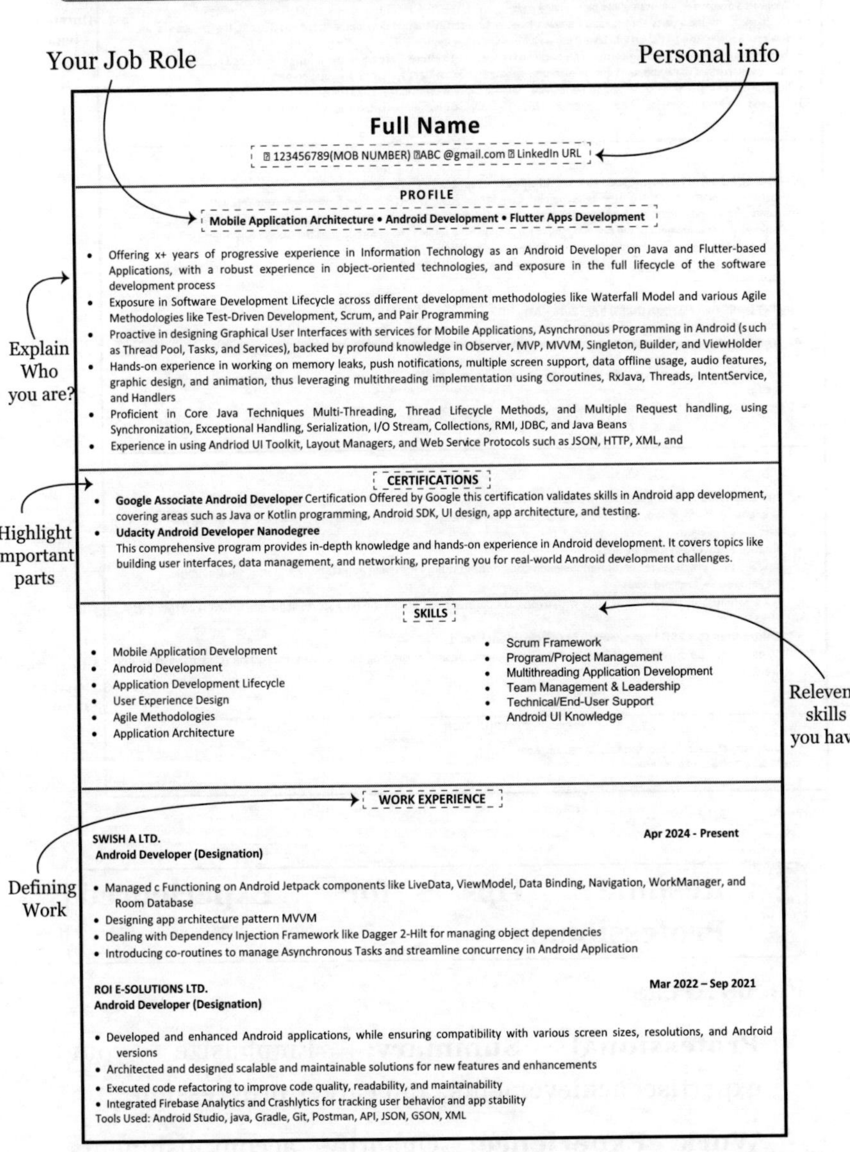

SINON TECH PVT. LTD.
Android Developer **Aug 2021 – Oct 2020**

- Harmonized with cross-functional teams with a view to define, design, and ship new features
- Translated design and wireframe into high-quality code
- Functioned with third-party libraries and frameworks generally used in Android development, such as Retrofit, Dagger, RxJava, etc.
- Dealt with responsive UI design and layout using Flutter's widget system
- Acquired knowledge in Firebase platform for backend services like Firestore, Firebase Authentication, and Cloud Functions
- Introduced custom UI components and animations applying Flutter's widget system and animation APIs
- Integrated RESTful APIs for obtaining and displaying dynamic content using Retrofit and Gson

Tools Used: Android Studio, java, IntelliJ, Postman, SQL, HTML, XML, Github, Bitbucket, Gitlab

PROJECTS

HEALTH EQUALS WEALTH (SINON TECH PVT. LTD.) | Jul 2017 – Sept 2020
HEW serves as a platform allowing users to accomplish their fitness goals, while facilitating posting achievements with options for likes, comments, shares, live streaming, connecting with peers, synchronizing fitness data, and participating in the AWS Affiliate program

- Initiated the development of the Android mobile application from scratch and launched it on the Google Play Store
- Introduced all the features mentioned above and implemented them on the mobile side
- Incorporated client feedback throughout the process, and handled bug-fixing/troubleshooting tasks to ensure a seamless user experience

VIMAKET (PARSHWA TECHNOLOGIES) | Apr 2016 – May 2017
Vimaket is a shopping destination, offering a large range of functionalities like Wishlist, Add to Cart, Shopping Bag, Address Management, User Profiles, and a seamless Checkout process, along with a Cash-on-Delivery payment option, just like other shopping apps

- Functioned with a small team of 2 Android Developers, and undertook the development of the application using Android Studio and Git
- Elevated the concept to life and launched it on the Google Play Store

ACCOMPLISHMENTS

- **Increased App User Engagement by 40%**
  Implemented efficient app features and enhanced UI/UX design, resulting in a significant increase in active user retention and daily engagement.
- **Reduced App Crash Rate by 30%**
  Applied best practices for error handling and code optimization, improving app stability and user satisfaction.
- **Developed 5+ Android Apps**
  Successfully launched multiple apps with over 10,000 downloads on Google Play Store, achieving an average rating of 4.5 stars.
- **Contributed to a 25% Improvement in Development Speed**
  Streamlined app development by introducing modular code and optimizing build processes, cutting release cycles by one week.

EDUCATION

- University of West London, London, United Kingdom
  M.Sc. in Software Engineering 2024

Writing Duration build trust

Add metrics to create an impact

3.5 Resume Tips for Experienced Professionals

Focus Areas

- **Professional Summary:** Emphasize your expertise, achievements, and career progression.
- **Work Experience:** Quantify accomplishments (e.g., "Increased sales by 30%").

- **Tailored Keywords:** Align your skills and experience with the job description.

Example:

Professional Summary: Results-driven marketing manager with over 8 years of experience in leading digital campaigns and increasing brand visibility. Proven track record in achieving a 25% increase in customer engagement through targeted strategies.

Skills

- **Digital Marketing:** SEO, PPC, Social Media Strategy
- **Tools:** Google Analytics, HubSpot, Salesforce
- **Leadership:** Team management, strategic planning

Work Experience: Marketing Manager | ABC Corp | 2018–Present

- Led a team of 10 to execute multi-channel marketing campaigns, resulting in a 25% increase in engagement.
- Streamlined marketing operations, reducing costs by 15%.

NOTE: Always use metrics in your work experience section to create an impact.

3.6 Sample Professional Summaries for Common Job Roles for Working Professionals

1. Software Engineer

Dynamic software engineer with 5+ years of experience in developing scalable web applications and working across the full software development lifecycle. Proficient in Java, Python, and cloud technologies, with a proven track record of reducing system downtime by 30% through process improvements.

2. Data Analyst

Detail-oriented data analyst with 3 years of experience in interpreting and analyzing data to drive business solutions. Skilled in SQL, Tableau, and Python, with a history of improving operational efficiency by leveraging data-driven insights.

3. Project Manager

Certified Project Manager (PMP) with 7 years of experience in successfully managing cross-functional teams and delivering projects on time and within budget. Expertise in Agile methodologies and risk management, resulting in a 20% improvement in project delivery metrics.

4. HR Professional

Experienced HR specialist with 6+ years of experience in talent acquisition, employee relations, and organizational development. Adept at implementing HR policies that increased employee satisfaction scores by 15% year over year.

5. Sales Manager

Goal-oriented sales manager with over 8 years of experience in driving revenue growth and leading high-performing sales teams. Demonstrated success in exceeding sales targets by 25% through strategic market penetration and relationship management.

Sample Professional Summaries for Common Job Roles for Freshers

1. Software Developer

Professional Summary: Enthusiastic and detail-oriented Computer Science graduate with a strong foundation in programming languages like Java, Python, and C++. Experienced in developing web-based applications through academic projects and internships. Adept at problem-solving and eager to contribute to innovative software solutions in a collaborative environment.

2. Marketing Coordinator

Professional Summary: Result-driven Marketing graduate with hands-on experience in social media management, content creation, and analytics through internships. Skilled in leveraging tools like Google Analytics and Canva to design marketing campaigns. Passionate about creating impactful marketing strategies to enhance brand visibility and audience engagement.

3. Data Analyst

Professional Summary: Highly analytical and motivated Statistics graduate with expertise in data visualization and interpretation. Proficient in tools like Excel, Tableau, and Python for analyzing large datasets. Eager to utilize analytical skills to support data-driven decision-making and organizational growth.

4. HR Assistant

Professional Summary: Dynamic and people-oriented HR Management graduate with a strong understanding of recruitment processes, employee engagement, and HR software. Experienced in coordinating campus hiring events during internships and adept at maintaining employee records. Passionate about fostering a positive workplace culture.

5. Financial Analyst

Professional Summary: Diligent and detail-oriented Finance graduate with strong analytical and problem-solving skills. Proficient in financial modeling, budgeting, and forecasting using tools like Excel and Power BI. Interested in contributing to financial planning and analysis to drive organizational profitability.

6. Business Analyst

Professional Summary: Energetic and resourceful Management graduate with a strong aptitude for analyzing business operations and implementing process improvements. Proficient in SQL, PowerPoint, and flowchart tools for presenting insights. Committed to delivering actionable business solutions and enhancing client satisfaction.

Watch detailed videos on crafting an ATS-friendly resume | Scan here ↓

Soft Skills that you must mention on your CV | Scan here ↓

3.7 ATS-Friendly Resumes: Myths busted

1. Ideal Resume Length

The ideal length of your resume depends on your experience level. **For freshers and early-career professionals, one page is sufficient. For experienced professionals with significant accomplishments, a two-page resume is acceptable.** Try not to exceed the length of the resume to more than two pages. Ensure every detail is relevant and adds value.

2. How Many Resumes Do You Need?

If you are applying for different job roles, one resume will not suffice. **You need separate resumes tailored for each job role.** For example, if a candidate is applying for both finance and marketing roles, they need to create two different resumes. A generic resume will never yield the desired results. Moreover, customize each resume by tailoring your skills, keywords, and accomplishments to match the specific job description. A tailored resume demonstrates your genuine interest and significantly improves your chances of getting shortlisted.

3. Should You Include a Photo?

In most cases, it's better to skip including a photo unless explicitly requested by the job posting. Photos can introduce unconscious bias and are generally unnecessary for ATS compatibility.

4. What About Hobbies and Interests?

Include hobbies and interests only if they are directly relevant to the role or demonstrate unique skills, such as leadership or teamwork. For example, if you're applying for a team-based role, mentioning your participation in sports teams could add value.

5. Should You List All Jobs?

Focus on the most relevant jobs and experiences. If you've had a long career, it's not necessary to include every job you've ever held. Instead, highlight roles that showcase your expertise and align with the job you're applying for.

6. Should You Mention Career Gaps in Your Resume?

The short answer is no—you shouldn't directly state that you have gaps in your resume. Instead, focus on presenting your qualifications, skills, and achievements in a way that emphasizes your value as a candidate. Here's why and how to address gaps effectively:

Why Not Mention Gaps Directly?

1. **Avoid Negative Perceptions:** Highlighting gaps upfront can draw unnecessary attention to them, potentially making recruiters question your commitment or reliability before reviewing your actual qualifications.

2. **Focus on Positives:** A resume should showcase your strengths, not draw attention to perceived weaknesses.

How to Address Career Gaps?

- **Highlight Transferable Skills:** Focus on skills gained during your career gap that are relevant to the job. For example: mention training, courses completed, recent certifications etc.

By addressing gaps thoughtfully and strategically, you can guide the recruiter's attention to what truly matters—your ability to excel in the role.

Watch resume mistakes to avoid | Scan here ↓

Final Thoughts

An ATS-friendly resume increases your chances of being shortlisted and moves you closer to landing your dream job. Always tailor your resume to the job description, proofread for errors, and stay consistent with formatting. Whether you're a fresher or an experienced professional, these tips will help you craft a resume that stands out—both to the ATS and the hiring manager.

CHAPTER 4

ACING FREQUENTLY ASKED INTERVIEW QUESTIONS

4.1 SECTION 1: PERSONALITY

4.1.1 Can you tell me about yourself?

REMEMBER MY FORMULA – "SEA" TO ANSWER THIS QUESTION

Mention these 3 elements in your answer

S = Skills

E = Experience / Education

A = Accomplishments

Do's:	Don'ts:
• Match your skill set with the eligibility criteria mentioned in the JD	• Don't recite your resume
• Research about the company thoroughly	• Practice and don't memorize
• Make it crystal clear why you are interested for the position	• Avoid mentioning too much of personal information like – family, age, marital status, political or religious views
• Talk about what you can bring to the table that aligns with the role and company.	

Sample answer for Experienced Candidates (with a few years of experience)

- Mention your College and Qualification
- Use work adjectives to describe yourself
- Experience and skills relevant to the job description
- Accomplishments

Sample Answer 1 (Role: Accounting Executive)

I graduated from The Hindu College, Delhi University. I was previously working with XYZ company as a diligent ***(you can use any powerful work adjective)*** accounting executive. I have 3 years of experience in the field of accountancy. I am experienced in handling the auditing process, providing client support and understanding requirements between the client and the company. I would love to mention that I started my career as an accounting executive but after a year I was promoted to X position. I have the skills and the experience that you are looking for, especially in leading and coordinating teams.

Examples of Work adjectives

1. Productive
2. Creative
3. Innovative
4. Committed
5. Adaptive
6. Competent
7. Hard-working

8. Passionate
9. Motivated

Sample Answer 2 (Role: Sales Manager) (If you have 5+ years of work experience)

I'm a committed sales manager with an experience of 8 years working with ABC company. In these 8 years I have gained experience in handling difficult clients, meeting deadlines and increasing the sales of the company. I was awarded as the best employee as I managed to increase the sales by 20% and bring in 3 Million Dollar worth of new business to the organisation.

Sample Answer 3 (Role: Software Engineer)

(If you have completed relevant certification courses)

I'm a motivated person with an experience of 3 years working with OPPO Mobile as a software engineer. I have also had the opportunity to lead two projects with Z Company. I am a productive person and to gain extra knowledge I have also completed an ABC course from Coursera. I understand that a major part of this role focuses on leading mobile development teams, which my previous job has certainly prepared me for. I can assure you that I will be able to add a noteworthy contribution if you decide to take me on board.

Sample Answer 4 (Role: Generic)

Note: This sample answer can easily be used for any job role.

Make sure to tailor it as per your requirements.

My name is [Your Name], and I have over [X years] of experience in [Your Field/Industry], specializing in [Your Key Expertise]. I graduated with a degree in [Your Degree] from [Your University], which laid the foundation for my career in this field.

Professional Background:

"Currently, I work at [Your Current Company] as a [Your Job Title], where I am responsible for [Mention 2-3 key responsibilities or accomplishments]. For instance, I successfully [Highlight a specific achievement, such as improving processes, exceeding targets, or leading a team/project]. Before this, I held a position at [Previous Company], where I [Mention a key contribution or role]."

Key Skills and Strengths:

Throughout my career, I've developed strong skills in [Mention 2-3 relevant skills, such as project management, data analysis, client relationship management, etc.]. My ability to [Highlight a key strength or soft skill, such as problem-solving, leadership, or communication] has helped me consistently deliver impactful results.

Why You're Here?

I am now looking to leverage my experience and skills in a role like this one at [Company Name]. I'm particularly drawn to [Mention something specific about the company or role, such as its culture, projects, or growth opportunities], and I believe my background aligns well with the challenges and goals of this position."

Closing:

Outside of work, I enjoy [Share a brief personal interest or hobby, like reading, traveling, or volunteering], which helps me stay balanced and creative. I'm excited about the opportunity to contribute to your team and continue growing professionally.

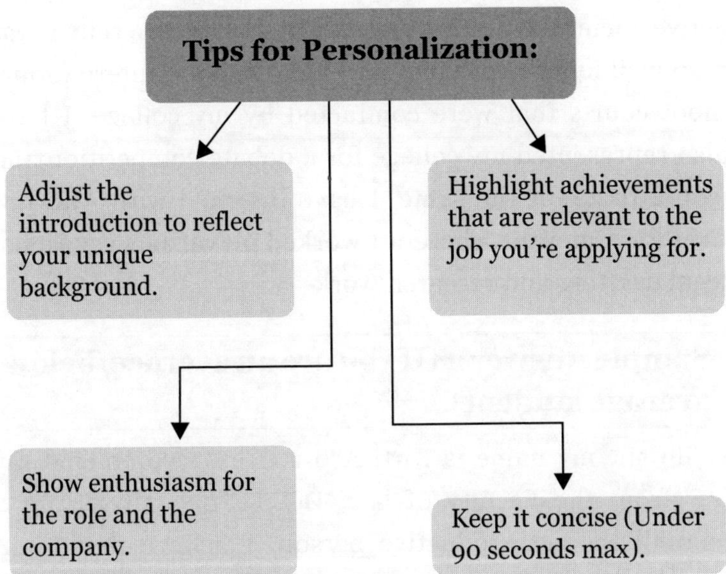

Tell me about yourself (Fresher)

- Mention your college / degree
- Internships / projects
- Skills and interests that are relevant to the job description
- Why are you a great fit?

Sample Answer 1 (If you hold a strong academic record)

Hello sir, my name is Kirti Arora (Mention your full name). I have completed my Law from Faculty of Law, Delhi University (Mention your college/university). Criminal Law has always been my favourite subject. Overall I have scored 75%. During my college I was an active member of the moot court society wherein I was responsible for managing and handling the international moot courts that were conducted by my college. I have also represented my college for a debate competition and won a prize for the same. I have interned with ABC law firm for 3 months wherein I worked on various aspects of legal drafting and research work.

Sample Answer 2 (If you are an average/below average student)

Hello sir, my name is Kirti Arora. I have completed my law from the Faculty of law, Delhi University. I am a committed and productive person. I believe that I can survive in a fast-paced environment. I am really looking forward to work here. I can assure you that I will be an asset to this firm if I am chosen to contribute. I believe that my commitment and motivation will ensure that I quickly become a valued member of your team.

Sample Answer 3 (Job Role : Generic)

Introduction: Thank you for the opportunity! My name is [Your Name], and I recently graduated with a degree in [Your Degree] from [Your University]. During my studies, I developed a strong interest in [Your Field/Area of Interest], which has motivated me to pursue a career in this area.

Academic Background and Projects: During my academic journey, I actively participated in [Mention relevant academic projects, internships, or coursework]. For example, I worked on [Briefly describe a key project or internship], where I [Explain what you did and achieved, e.g., developed solutions, learned specific tools/ technologies, or improved processes]. This experience gave me hands-on exposure to [Highlight skills or tools gained, e.g., teamwork, technical tools, problem-solving].

Key Skills and Strengths: I have developed strong skills in [Mention 2-3 key skills relevant to the role, such as data analysis, communication, coding, etc.]. Additionally, I take pride in being [Highlight a soft skill or strength, such as a quick learner, adaptable, or detail-oriented], which helps me approach challenges effectively.

Why You're Here: I am eager to start my professional journey and contribute to [Company Name] by applying my skills and passion for [Mention something relevant to the role or company, such as innovation, problem-solving, or teamwork]. I am particularly impressed by [Highlight something specific about the company, like its culture, recent achievements, or mission].

Closing: Outside of academics, I enjoy [Briefly mention a hobby or interest, such as playing a sport, volunteering, or exploring technology], which helps me stay balanced and motivated. I am excited about the opportunity to learn and grow as part of your team.

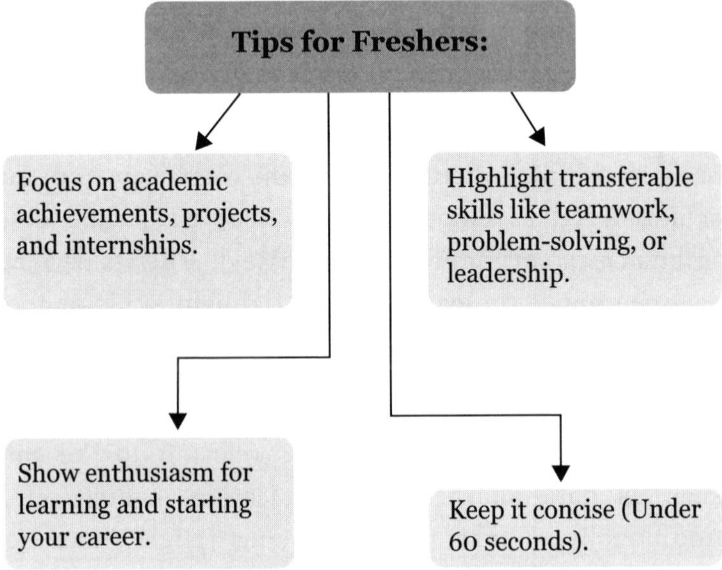

Watch detailed video on answering "Tell me about yourself in an interview" | Scan Here ↓

4.1.2 What are your strengths and weaknesses?

What does the interviewer want to know?

- Are you aware of your weaknesses?
- What have you done to overcome your weaknesses?
- How can your strengths help the company to grow?
- Do you know yourself well and care to learn from your experiences?

Approach to answer this question

<u>**Common Mistake**</u>

Giving one-line answers and not backing it up with an example

- **For example:**
  - ↳ My weakness is that I am very emotional. ✖
  - ↳ My strength is that I am very motivated and self-driven. ✖

<u>**Approach to answer this question**</u>

Make a list of your strengths and weaknesses keeping in mind the job description.

What are your strengths?

Let's divide our strengths into 3 categories

Knowledge based	Soft Skills	Personality Traits
• Education	• Problem-solving	• Collaborative
• Experience	• Negotiation	• Diligent
• Internships	• Communication Skills	• Creative
• Projects	• Leadership skills	• Adaptable
• Freelance work	• Management Skills	• Fast-Learner
• Certifications	• Time management	• Organized
• Languages	• Stress management	• Resilient
	• Interpersonal Skills	• Strategic

Experienced Candidate

Sample Answer 1

My greatest strength is **flexibility to handle change.** As a customer service manager at my last job, I was able to turn around a negative working environment and develop a supportive team.

Sample Answer 2

My biggest strength is my **communication** and **networking skills**. As a sales executive it's part of my job to understand the needs of my clients and maintain proper transparency among all the team members. I am proud to mention that I have always been successful at it. This has not only helped me to deliver best results but also maintain a great professional network.

Fresher

Sample Answer 1

My greatest strength is that I have a **solid work ethic**. The projects and internships that I have done have trained me well to meet the deadlines. I have always been appreciated by my teachers for completing the assignments well ahead of schedule.

Sample Answer 2

My greatest strength is that I am a **committed and disciplined person**. During my internships, I was fully committed to learning as much as possible. I strongly believe, especially during college life, that our project work and internships help us to build a strong foundation to excel in our careers. I have always been appreciated by my teachers and seniors for my sincerity.

Weaknesses

Knowledge based	Soft Skills	Personality traits
• Unfamiliar • Technical Skills	• Creativity • Delegation • Spontaneity • Public- Speaking skills	• Self-criticism • Procrastinating • Impatient • Shy • Lack of self-confidence • Indecisive • Asking for help

Frame your weakness in a positive light and focus on what have you done to overcome it

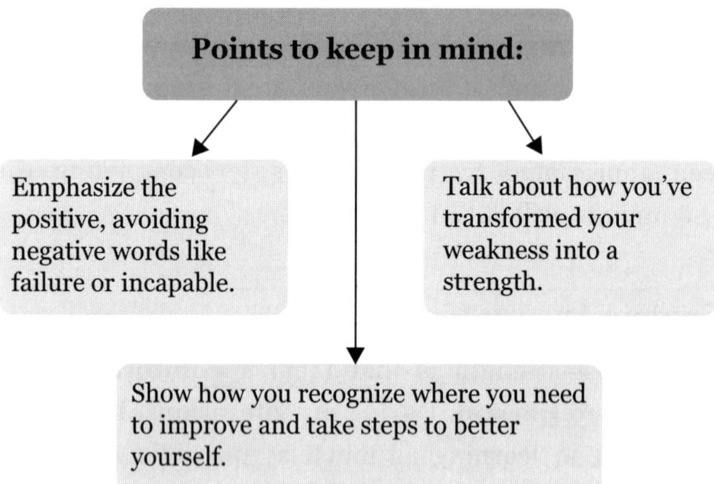

What are ways you can improve yourself to address a weakness?

- Enrol in a course or training program to develop the necessary skills.
- Utilize tools and technology like apps to manage your time, schedule breaks, or enhance collaboration.
- Seek guidance from a mentor who can provide insights and support for your growth.
- Participate in volunteer opportunities to gain hands-on experience and strengthen specific skills.
- Join professional organizations or industry associations to expand your network and stay updated on best practices.

Sample Answer 1

Although I always **meet my deadlines**, I used to have a problem with procrastination, and I'd end up working really long hours as a deadline approached. So, I decided that I needed to deal with the issue, and I took classes on project management and time management. I learned how to organize my days and attack bigger projects in manageable chunks. Now, I always map out my plan beforehand as soon as I get a new assignment, and now I often beat my deadlines.

Sample Answer 2

My biggest weakness is at times **I overburden myself with work.** I have sincerely worked towards this by prioritizing what is most important and strictly working according to that. I believe chalking out a plan and working according to the time table helps a lot.

4.1.3 What are your hobbies?

Other ways to ask this question is

- What do you like to do outside of work?
- What do you do in your free time?

Common Mistakes

Avoid irrelevant statements: I only like to work or I don't have any hobbies.

Correct approach to answer this question

Step 1: Select applicable hobbies and interests

Some common hobbies to mention during an interview include:

- Travel
- Volunteering, community service or charity work
- Sports such as competing on a team or in a league, hiking or other exercise
- Creative arts, including writing, music, painting and crafts
- Listening to podcasts
- Reading books

Step 2 : Mention what skills have you acquired from these activities

Some options might include:

- Planning and organization skills
- Leadership skills
- Communication and interpersonal skills
- Teamwork
- Determination and commitment
- Creative thinking and problem solving
- Patience
- Adaptability

Final step: Find relations between your hobbies and the job

Now, there are many companies which engage in outdoor activities for team outings.

If you are a fresher this can be a great example for you:-

Sample Answer 1 (Playing Sports)

I have **played sports** since high school. I was in fact the captain of my team. As a captain I have always **encouraged** other players to understand the importance of **discipline** and **time**. During my captaincy, I always used to urge them to come an hour before and practice the game. **My experience** as a team captain has provided me with opportunities **to conduct training sessions and boost morale of my team members in tough situations.**

And to keep the interview interactive you can also say:-

"I actually saw that you had a field day for your last company event? Do you commonly do outdoor activities for team outings"?

Sample Answer 2 (Traveling)

I love travelling and I try to take a trip every season. Travelling allows me to adapt myself to new situations, mix up with people from different backgrounds and I absolutely love that. I am always the planner in the group and everyone loves the way I plan out the days so that we don't miss on anything. In fact, I believe it's because of my planning and organizational skills that anyone who takes a trip with me enjoys to the fullest.

Sample Answer 3 (Reading Books, Working Out & Cooking)

My hobbies are reading books and working out. Along with this, I also like cooking. While researching the company, I got to know about the in-house gym. Having a gym in a workplace is a great idea as employees can get to know each other better on a casual level apart from their official roles.

Sample Answer 4 (Learning New Languages)

I like learning new skills and recently I have been interested in exploring different languages as they help me explore new cultures around the world. I started learning French online and I have already cleared the beginner level. In a few weeks, I will be completing my course and will also get a certificate for the same. On weekends, I like to watch French Movies with subtitles and this has really helped me to strengthen my French vocabulary.

4.1.4 What is unique about you?

Other ways of asking this question: -

1. What sets you apart?
2. What makes you different from other candidates?
3. Why should we pick you?
4. What makes you special?

What does the interviewer want to know?

- What skills, qualities and experiences make you the best candidate for this job?
- Have you done your research on the job role?

Approach to answer this question:-

- Try not to concentrate too much on the word 'unique', the employer is not expecting you to come up with an answer that they've never heard of.

Examples of what all you can say:-

- A time when you were praised by your manager or a colleague for something you accomplished or completed particularly well.
- Any positive characteristic or personality trait.
- Any non-academic or extracurricular achievements, or an occasion where you have resolved an issue or helped someone.

Sample Answer 1 (Fast-Learner) (Experienced Candidates)

The unique skill set that I will bring to your workplace is my ability to learn quickly with minimum supervision. Having worked with _______ company before, I am happy to take on additional responsibilities outside my "remit". I have read the job description and as you require the candidate to do _____ and _____ I will be able to contribute effectively.

Sample Answer 2 (Innovative / Creative) (Freshers)

I strongly believe, one of my main qualities that makes me unique and different from other candidates is my ability to come up with innovative and creative ideas to complete my tasks. During my university period, my ideas were the final choice in the group projects. For example, I would love to share my recent project work with you. In this project, I was responsible to do _______ and ______. I laid down an effective strategy to split the work according to everyone's skills and abilities. This helped our group to score pretty well.

Sample Answer 3 (Active Listening Skills) (Experienced Candidates)

I have great listening skills. I am always appreciated for this. I handle situations calmly with a level head. My friends and family often seek my advice to help them in stressful situations. In fact, I recently helped my teammate to get out of an awkward situation with an unhappy client. I made him realise how important it is for him to listen and understand the requirements of our clients to avoid such situations in future.

Sample Answer 4 (Risk-Taker) (Freshers + Experienced Candidates)

I am not afraid of trying new things. I love to explore and take calculated risks. I am an avid believer of the fact that stepping outside your comfort zone is always important if you want to excel.

4.1.5 Tell me about your goals?

What does the interviewer want to know?

- Do you have clarity of mind?
- Are you serious about your career?
- Are you going to stick with the company?

Correct approach to answer this question:-

- Research about the company's mission, vision & their requirements.
- Make sure to mention that your long term goals align with the company requirements.

Sample Answer 1 (Applying for entry-level position)

To begin with, my immediate goal is to gain valuable industry knowledge and experience. As this is an entry-level position, I hope to work for the company to gain new skills and develop an idea of how I can contribute to the organization.

Sample Answer 2 (Applying for management level position)

One of my goals is to serve as a role model for those I'm managing. I want to be a mentor to others and help them achieve their full potential. To do this, I intend to keep full coordination and transparency among all the team members.

Sample Answer 3 (Student/ Intern)

Role: Marketing

Well, I'll be graduating next year and I would love to start working in the marketing department of a company like yours right away. Apart from expanding my knowledge and experience in marketing, I also hope to enhance my communication and public speaking skills. I really want to be a proactive and valuable team member.

Sample Answer 4 (Students + Freshers)

Role: Generic

One thing that is definitely on my priority list is to enrol myself in X course. I do have knowledge around that. However, I am aware that if I will study X course in depth, it would serve as an additional advantage to contribute to your upcoming projects.

4.1.6 Where do you see yourself in 5 years?

What does the interviewer want to know?

- Are you focused and serious about your career?
- What are your long term goals?
- Will you stick with the company for a long run?

Approach to answer this question

- Show that you are ambitious and enthusiastic
- Mention realistic goals
- Align your long term goals with the company's needs

- Focus on mentioning that you plan to stick with the company and settle in with the company's culture.

Sample Answer 1 (Fresher)

Role: Generic

At present I aim to work at your company and learn new skills to grow in my career. I would definitely love to work at ______ position (mention one-two positions higher than what you are applying for) in the next 5 years after gaining good experience here. I have reviewed the job description and this company seems the right fit for me to achieve my long term goals.

Sample Answer 2 (Experienced professional)

Role: Generic

In the next 5-7 years, I see myself as leading a team. I have always enjoyed leadership skills in my career. I am confident that I have the skills to maintain coordination and lead a team with full motivation. In fact, I read in the job description about great leadership opportunities. It got me really excited to apply here and learn more about the same.

Same Answer 3 (Experienced Professional)

Role: Assistant Professor

I am looking forward to being a part of the teaching faculty at your school / college. Currently I am pursuing _______ to complete my training. In the next 5 years, I see myself more settled with all the required qualifications, ready to be part of your core faculty. I am sure I will be able to contribute in helping students to build their career. Afterall, teaching has always been my passion and I enjoy this profession to the fullest.

Sample Answer 4 (Experienced Professional)

Role: Sales Executive

As a sales executive I see myself taking up more responsibility and improving my skills to strengthen my relationship with customers and to meet sales quota with much more ease. I have seen in my previous job how my seniors used to take regular follow ups with the customers. I have always looked up to how their focus was always on providing best services to the customers. Being in this industry I truly value the importance of customer's feedback. I am sure I will be able to contribute more in the long run here.

Sample Answer 5 (Fresher)

Role: Social Media Manager

I would love to join in here as a social media manager and continue learning more about the digital space. So for 1-2 years I would love to contribute in creating content, managing posts and responding to your followers, across all the social channels of your company. Once I have got a good hold of it, in the next 3-5 years I would love to take more responsibility of helping the company to look for more opportunities to increase brand exposure. As a social media manager, I love to learn about the latest digital technologies and social trends. In fact I have also completed a digital marketing course which has given me a deeper insight of achieving marketing goals. I am really excited to contribute my skills to help the company ensure high levels of web traffic and customer engagement.

4.1.7 Why are you the best person for this job?

NOTE: This question is a variation of the most frequently asked interview question – Why should we hire you?

Correct approach to answer this question

- Match your qualifications to those listed in JD.
- Talk about your skill set

Sample Answer 1

My skill set is a perfect match for the job requirements. In particular, my communication skills and managerial experience make me an ideal candidate for the position.

Sample Answer 2

I have the ability to find my place within a group and support everyone's efforts. For example, my last job involved a lot of team projects. I read the JD for this company and as you require a candidate to work in large groups, I believe I will be a perfect match for this role.

Sample Answer 3

I am a **self-motivated person** who is willing to go above and beyond on any project, pushing to learn valuable skills in the stipulated time. I can assure you that I will be an asset to this company if I am chosen to contribute.

4.1.8 How would your friends describe you?

NOTE: This question helps the HR to understand what soft skills you will bring to the table.

TIP: The best tip is to "***Pick Likeable Traits***" and focus on the type of position you are applying for.

Sample Answer (Software Developer)

"My friends would describe me as an **optimist**. I never let little frustrations set me back and I'm always looking for solutions right away.

Sample Answer 2 (Human Resources Manager)

My friends would describe me as **helpful and communicative**. I don't really enjoy idle time, so when a friend needs help with something, they will always find me by their side. They would certainly say that I am a reliable and patient listener.

Sample Answer 3: Teacher

They'd say that I'm **compassionate and empathetic**. "They would also say I'm a curious person who loves to learn and share interesting stories.

Sample Answer 4 (Data Analyst)

They'd say that I am very **observant**. I pay a lot of attention to details. And I am glad that I am like this. As this has always helped me in my professional life.

4.1.9 How would your co-workers describe you?

Sample Answer 1

I am known best for being a **team-oriented leader**. One of my proudest moments was when one of my co-workers offered to write me a letter of recommendation because she admired my empathy and leadership during challenging projects.

Sample Answer 2

My colleagues have told me that they value my **reliability, punctuality and analytical mindset**. I always work to manage my time effectively so that I can help others with last-minute projects and spend extra time reviewing my work for accuracy.

4.2 SECTION 2: PROBLEM-SOLVING

1. Tell me about a challenge or conflict that you have faced at work / college and how you've dealt with it?
2. Tell me about a time you made a mistake and how you handled it?
3. Describe a project that was really difficult and tell me how you solved it.

4.2.1 Tell me about a challenge or conflict that you have faced at work / college and how you've dealt with it?

What does the interviewer want to know?

- How do you deal with stress?
- Want to assess your problem-solving skills
- Any client issues?
- Your patience levels
- How well do you work with the team?
- Interpersonal skills and how you manage with a conflict

Other ways this question can be asked are:-

- Tell me about an assignment when you had to work with someone difficult.
- Give an example of a time you had to respond to an unhappy customer or co-worker.
- Tell me about a time that you disagreed with a manager.

Correct approach to answer this question

Step 1: Make a list of challenges that you have faced at work

Common challenges at workplace

1. Meeting stressful deadlines
2. Unreasonable Clients
3. Difficult team / teammate
4. Disagreeable coworkers / manager

5. Fitting in (Figuring out how to be part of a new work culture)

Use the STAR method that I have taught you to answer this

1. **Situation** (Briefly explain the issue you were dealing with in a positive, constructive way)
2. **Task** (Describe your role in the situation)
3. **Action** (What did you do to resolve the conflict)
4. **Result** (Emphasize on what you learned and how your actions had a positive outcome)

Sample Answer 1 (Experienced Professionals) (Situation: Disagreement with a coworker)

Situation/Task

Once there was a teammate who was unable to meet the deadline of an important project. When I approached him about the same, he reacted defensively. I kept calm and acknowledged that the deadlines were challenging and asked how I could assist him in improving his performance. He calmed down and told me that he was involved in another project that was assigned to him last minute.

Action

I decided to hold a meeting with all the team members and came to the conclusion that to avoid such situations it's mandatory that proper communication is always maintained between all the team members.

We then discussed the importance of proper planning and organizing tasks in advance to ensure that deadlines are met. We also came up with solutions such as delegating tasks, setting up reminders, and getting help from each other when needed. Everyone agreed to the solutions, and we decided to implement them in order to avoid any future issues with meeting deadlines. Everyone was thankful for my initiative and agreed to work together for the success of our project.

Result

After that, all of us were able to meet the deadline successfully.

Sample Answer 2 (Experienced Professionals) (Situation: Disagreement with boss)

Situation/Task

I disagreed with my boss in a group meeting over how to help a client. To respect his position, I chose to not express my opinion in front of the team.

Action

Instead, I asked for a one-on-one meeting and told him politely why I disagreed with his decision. We were eventually able to find an amicable solution and provide the best services for the client. The one-on-one meeting was constructive, and I was pleased that we were able to work through our differences and come to a better solution together.

Result

I learned it is important to have the courage to stand up for what you believe in and have healthy debates with those around you, but also to remain respectful of their decisions.

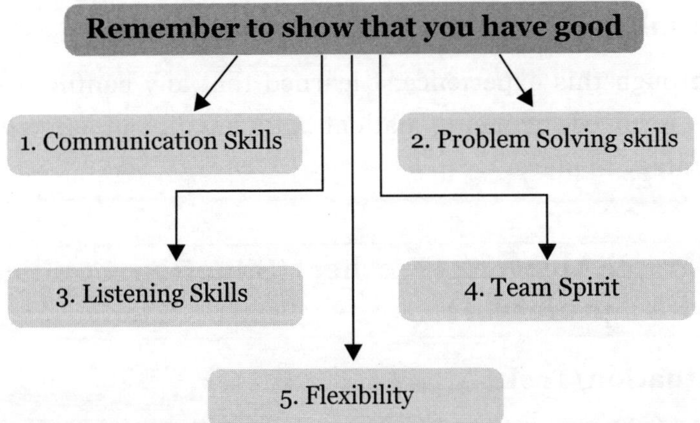

Sample Answer 3 (Experienced Professionals) (Situation: Teacher who had a conflict with a student's parent)

Situation/Task

I recently had a difficult situation with one of my student's parents who was concerned about their daughter's physics grades. The parent emailed the principal, stating that I wasn't doing enough to help the child.

Action

After speaking with the principal, I scheduled a one-on-one meeting with the parent. At first, they were quite aggressive, but I remained calm and listened to their concerns as they were worried about upcoming exams. Instead of focusing on why things weren't going right, I changed the focus of our meeting to how we could help their daughter improve her grades and came up with solutions that satisfied them.

Result

Through this experience, I learned that any conflict can be resolved by being patient and having an effective strategy in place.

Sample Answer 4 (Fresher) (Situation: Conflict with a professor)

Situation/Task

When I was in my second year of college, I had a professor for a History course who would often give unclear instructions for assignments and get frustrated by any questions that we asked. One day, we had to write a research paper, and the professor gave us a very vague set of instructions.

Action

When I approached him to ask for clarification, he became very defensive and started yelling at me. I kept calm and stood my ground, and politely but firmly reminded him that we were all here to learn and that it would be beneficial if he could provide more details on the assignment.

Result

The professor eventually calmed down and gave us clearer instructions on the assignment and apologized for his behaviour. Afterward, I felt proud of myself for standing up to him and making sure that everyone in the class understood what was expected of them.

4.2.2 Tell me about a time you made a mistake and how did you handle it?

- **What does the interviewer want to know?**
  - How do you handle challenges?
  - What are your weak spots?
  - What have you learnt from your mistakes?
- **Approach to answer this question**
  - Briefly explain what the mistake was, but don't keep on ranting about it.
  - Focus should be on how you handled the situation.
  - Keep your tone positive rather than apologetic.
  - The most important strategy is to ensure that you have maturity to benefit from your previous mistakes.
  - Don't blame your fellow coworkers. Rather focus on what measures you have taken to avert errors in future.

Examples of common professional mistakes

1. Communication Issues
2. Not delegating tasks

3. Not asking enough questions
4. Not following up with customers
5. Overlooking important details in a project

Sample Answer 1 (Mistake: Communication Issues) (Experienced Professionals)

I am the kind of person who learns from every mistake. In my previous company, I was already working on a crucial project and in the meantime I was allotted another project. Instead of having an open discussion with my boss I burned myself out. Even after working for extra hours, I realized if I do not communicate this issue to my boss, I will not be able to meet the deadline. So, before I lost more time, I took my boss into the loop. He was in fact very encouraging and appreciated my dedication towards the work. He assigned another coworker to help me with the project. I have realized since then it's important to maintain transparency and proper communication with your seniors and bosses.

Sample Answer 2 (Mistake: Not delegating tasks) (Experienced Professionals)

When I joined my previous company as an XYZ (mention your role) (for example: Assistant Manager), I was always under a constant pressure to impress my boss. I ended up taking more work than I could manage. In spite of having a supportive team I choose not to delegate work and micro manage everything. As a result, my days at work used to be overwhelming and stressful. I spoke about the same to my senior and she made me realize that I have coworkers for a reason. She helped me to understand that in order to learn new things and balance my workload, it's often necessary to ask for help. I followed her advice and started giving my team more responsibilities. I ended up producing a better quality of work while my team also had the opportunity to grow better in their roles.

Note: Fresh Graduates can also use Sample Answer 2. Just change the first sentence as , "When I joined as an intern in XYZ company....

Sample Answer 3 (Mistake: Not asking enough questions) (Fresh Graduates)

During my internship, I was hesitant to ask questions, often feeling overwhelmed. During a performance review, my seniors noted that I wasn't learning enough. They encouraged me to be more inquisitive and vocal with any issues or doubts that I had. After their advice, I began writing down any questions or problems I encountered while working on a project in order to gain more clarity and growth in my role. I also made sure to take on any additional tasks that were available, so I could gain more hands-on experience and learn different skills. This gave me the confidence to step out of my comfort zone and become more engaged in my work. Ultimately, these changes resulted in a better understanding of the company and its operations, which in turn led to a successful end to my internship.

Sample Answer 4 (Not following up with customers) (Experienced Professionals)

When I joined my previous company I wasn't meeting the sales number. I decided to reach out to my manager and ask for his opinion. Although he encouraged me by saying that I am a competent person, I also need to work on taking follow ups from the customers. I took his advice and my numbers doubled. This experience has taught me that as a sales manager regular follow ups with the customers gives an impression that you care about them. That is why customers stick with your business for a longer period of time as you are always available.

Sample Answer 5 (Overlooking important details in a project) (Experienced Professionals)

As an editor, I was responsible for proofreading a story which was to be published in our weekly magazine. Unfortunately, I overlooked that the pages of the story were numbered incorrectly. This mistake went unnoticed until we had already sent the story to the printer. Fearing that this could disrupt the alignment of numbers with our table of contents, I quickly contacted the printer who thankfully had not yet started printing our pages. The mistake was fixed, and I learned my lesson: never overlook even small details when proofreading anything as a final draft. To prevent this mistake from happening in the future, I created a checklist for my team and myself to follow while proofreading stories. The checklist includes double-checking for errors such as incorrect page numbering, typos, grammatical mistakes and formatting errors.

4.2.3 Describe a project that was really difficult and tell me how you solved it?

- **What does the interviewer want to know?**

↳ Are you a performer?

↳ Can you handle work stress?

Approach to answer this question

Briefly explain the challenges you faced and then shift the focus to the results you achieved

Sample Answer 1 (Freshers + Experienced Professionals) (Generic)

I would love to share this with you. I was working on a _______ project. In this project I was responsible to do _______ and ________ . I found it difficult in the beginning because_________. I would say my patience level and my nature to keep myself grounded in such challenging situations got me through.

Sample Answer 2 (Fresher)

In the first week of my internship with XYZ company, a client asked for a major change on their website just a few days before its launch. There was a lot of chaos in the office. As I was just an intern no one was eager to include me in their teams as they were on tight deadlines. I took initiatives on my own and decided to stay and help the team anyway. I wasn't trained in the tools they used, but I offered to test the website. I tested every page over and over until all errors got fixed. After that, the manager decided to include me in the next project as a trainee. That was a real proud moment for me.

Sample Answer 3 (Experienced Professional)

When I was working at ABC company, I was leading a project. (Explain the project). It was a bit challenging because the project was assigned to me very late. My boss told me that the deadlines are tight and it's important that we deliver our best because the client was very important to us. I selected 7 co-workers and delegated them different tasks according to their skill set and capabilities. We all worked overtime and were able to complete the project on time. My boss appreciated me for my planning, communication and leadership skills.

4.3 SECTION 3: DECISION-MAKING

1. Can you explain why your grades were so low in college?
2. Why did you choose this career?
3. Why is there a gap in your employment?
4. Why are you changing your career path/ industry?
5. Why are you changing your job so soon?
6. Are you willing to relocate?
7. Would you consider taking less pay than you made in your last job?

4.3.1 Can you explain why your grades were so low in college?

- **What does the interviewer want to know?**
  - ↳ Reason why you scored less marks?
  - ↳ Are you serious and focused now?
- **Approach to answer this question**
  - ↳ Briefly explain the reason why you scored less marks
  - ↳ Shift the focus on your achievements and accomplishments
  - ↳ Don't blame the faculty
  - ↳ Don't make excuses. For e.g.: I scored less marks because I was always busy playing basketball. Rather focus on how co-curricular activities are an important aspect of your personality.
- **Common Reasons for low grades**
  - ↳ Working part time along with college
  - ↳ Health issues
  - ↳ Active in sports
  - ↳ Too much focus on co-curricular activities
  - ↳ Lack of focus on studies

Sample Answer 1 (Reason – Working part time along with college)

I accept the fact that my grades are lower than required. Reason being, I could not extensively focus on my classes full-time because I was doing a part-time job as ______ . It certainly affected my grades but it has given me a lot of practical experience. I feel more prepared and confident to take this job full time now because of the same.

Sample Answer 2 (Reason – Health Issue)

My grades were affected because of my health issues. I was struggling a lot to concentrate on my studies because I was physically / mentally not doing well. I am certainly healthy now and I am excited to work hard and grow my career working with your company.

Sample Answer 3 (Reason - Active in Sports)

I understand that my grades were low in college as I was a student who was quite active in sports. I have represented my college in ____ and ____ tournament. Although my active participation in sports affected my grades, I was able to build my skills in many other ways. It has trained me well to work in a team with coordination and discipline. I am now really looking forward to starting my career with your company.

Sample Answer 4 (Reason - Too much focus on co-curricular activities)

I have not been able to score high grades in college as I was deeply involved in organizing college fests, competitions and all the major events. I have been an active student throughout my college life and all these activities have given me real life experiences from meeting deadlines, working with limited budgets and most importantly being disciplined and organized. I have the same clarity in my mind as I had in my college which is to focus on the task at hand and deliver it with perfection. It will be great if I am given an opportunity to contribute to your company.

Sample Answer 5 (Lack of focus on your studies)

I accept the fact that my grades are lower than required, reason being, my lack of focus on academics and more inclination towards practical aspects. I truly understand the value and importance of studies and grades but I was more occupied in learning practical and hands-on skills. I have done ____ and ____ courses with a mindset that I want to build a career out of this. I am pretty confident that if I am given a chance to contribute, I will put my best foot forward to achieve good results.

4.3.2 Why did you choose this career?

Other ways to ask this question:

- Why did you decide to become a ______?
- What factors influenced you to choose this career path?

What does the interviewer want to know?

- How motivated and committed are you?
- Who motivated you?
- How focused are you?
- Was it always your plan or was it just a random decision?

Reasons for choosing a career

- You've always had an interest in this career or job from a young age.
- You have a parent, friend or family member who encouraged you to get into it, and you found out that you like it a lot.
- You had a professor or teacher who encouraged you to get into this career field.

Approach to answer this question

- Think about all the positive factors that influenced your decision to choose "x" career path.
- Show your passion and interest for the career. Talk about the internships, summer programmes, certification courses, any workshops if attended etc.
- Talk about the research that you did before choosing this career. (this really impresses the interviewer)

Sample Answer 1 (Fresher) (Role: Lawyer)

I committed myself to becoming a lawyer because law is one profession that encourages discussions and arguments to unfold truth and deliver justice. It has always fascinated me. I was very clear on becoming a lawyer and also researched well about its scope. In addition to this my teachers and parents were also very helpful in providing me with proper guidance on choosing this career path. I also attended webinars on legal drafting and I am sure under your guidance I will be able to unravel my skills. I would love to mention that my father always tells me that he sees a great lawyer in me.

Sample Answer 2 (Fresher) (Role: Engineer)

"There were many influences that went into my decision to select this career field. One of my early mentors was a business friend of my mother's, who is a successful mechanical engineer. She encouraged me to explore opportunities in this field. She pointed me in the right direction to explore the possibilities. But it was the combination of my career research along with my professors who helped to solidify my decision. My internship last summer helped me to get an inside view into the scope and opportunities in this field."

Sample Answer 3 (Fresher) (Sector: IT field)

"I chose to work in IT because I've always been genuinely interested in technology, particularly how quickly technology is advancing. I also did quite a bit of research before choosing this career while I was in college, and it seemed to have high job satisfaction and great long-term prospects for career growth. So, I felt that this career fits my personal interests and also my career goals."

Sample Answer 4 (Experienced Professionals) (Sector: Science field)

To be honest, when I entered college I was quite unsure about this career. But I had a great professor who made biology a really fun subject. I always looked up to him and admire him till date. He has been a real motivation. He had previously worked with a big pharma company so he had real motivating stories to share what it's like to be a scientist. I decided to choose this as my career path and since then I have worked with two different fortune 500 companies in R&D and choose to continue this career with great enthusiasm.

4.3.3 Why is there a gap in your employment?

In discussing any sabbatical you might have taken, start by explaining the reasons that led you to take the time off. Then explain the ways in which you grew from the experience personally and professionally. Portray it the correct way, these kinds of resumé gaps can actually give a positive outlook to your CV, if you choose to use them correctly.

What does the interviewer want to know?

- What was the reason?
- Are you fully prepared to get back to work?

Approach to answer this question

- Explain the reason for the gap
- Don't appear awkward, answer the question confidently
- Don't spend too much time explaining the reason
- Rather focus on the skills you have learned during the break
- Assure it won't happen again

Common Reasons for taking a break

- Health issues
- Family emergencies

- To study further
- If you voluntarily took some time off
- Maternity / Paternity leave
- Wanted to start your own business

Sample Answer 1 (Health issues)

I took a break from work due to a medical condition. I was diagnosed with _____ and was recommended to take rest. However, I used to utilize my time by keeping myself up to date with new trends emerging in my field. I also completed a course on ABC to upskill my knowledge. I was eagerly waiting to recover and to get back to work. I am now completely healthy both physically and mentally and I am really excited to start a new job.

Sample Answer 2 (Family emergencies)

I had to leave my previous organization due to a family emergency. Since _ months, I have been taking care of my family. It was that phase of my life when my family needed me the most so I decided to take a break and work things out. As I always knew it's a testing time for me and my family and eventually this time is going to pass, I constantly kept myself in touch with the recent trends related to my field. However, thankfully the problem has been taken care of & concrete steps have been taken to ensure no such emergencies arise in the future. Keeping all that in the past, I sit here in this interview with the right skills & zeal to start working again as soon as possible.

Sample Answer 3 (To study Further)

While working in my previous organization, I identified a few fields wherein I wanted to learn more. Since that wasn't possible to achieve while working full time, I decided to quit my job & study more to fulfil those gaps. I have finally completed _____ degree now.

I feel grateful because I have learned many new things in my field and feel that my skills have sharpened & I can be much more productive professionally.

Sample Answer 4 (If you voluntarily took some time off) (Travelling)

I took six months out to immerse myself in a different culture and I feel I've not only gained a new perspective, but I've also learned some valuable life lessons. It was good to experience different countries and learn about different things. I am grateful I did this because I have learned a lot in this process. I'm now ready to start focusing on my career.

Sample Answer 5 (Maternity / Paternity leave)

I had to take a break from my career as I was focused on being a full time mother / father. My spouse and I did not have any help. So I decided to take a break for a few months. On the contrary to this, we both are focused and career oriented people. I always knew that I wanted to get back to work soon. Thankfully we have found the right house help who takes care of our child and is responsible enough with her duties. This has enabled me to shift my focus back to my career and here I am to start again with full energy and enthusiasm.

Sample Answer 6 (Wanted to start your own business)

I had to take a break because I was working on ______ project (briefly explain the project). I have 7 years of experience working with XYZ company. I have learned a lot during my job. Perhaps, I always wanted to test the waters for myself and see if I can be successful at it. So I decided to take a break for 1 year. Unfortunately, due to cut throat competition the plan failed. But I still have no regrets, as during this time I have learnt a lot, especially how to do competitive market research and build a strong team. I feel grateful that I have gained hands-on experience of building something from scratch.

4.3.4 Why are you changing your Career Path/ Industry?

What does the interviewer want to know?

- What is the reason behind the switch?
- Are you clear about your goals?

Approach to answer this question

- Mention one or two skills that you have developed in your previous role that will help you in the new role.
- You can also mention your passion about the current role that you are applying for. If you are pressed to give reasons for such a career switch, be prepared for that.

Reasons for changing your Career path/ Industry

- Personal Interest and passion.
- You have discovered you can perform better in the new role.
- You are unsatisfied in your current career.
- Work flexibility is another important factor that influences career change.
- You have developed an interest in an evolving field.
- You feel your skills and values are undervalued.

Sample Answer 1 (Fresher) (Situation – A lawyer who wants to become an English Teacher)

I graduated as a lawyer and I have really enjoyed learning and studying law. There are many important skills that I have developed as a lawyer. For example, I have great communication and public speaking skills. I have discovered that these skills will be an additional factor to help me grow as a teacher. If studying law was my choice, becoming a teacher is my passion. And I strongly believe, when you follow your passion, you always get success.

Sample Answer 2 (Experienced Professional) (Role: Generic)

I have experience in ______ (current career) field for ________ years and I have enjoyed every bit of it. I have decided to switch to ______ (new career) because I am not finding this career challenging enough. However, I don't regret my choices, as the skills that I have developed in my current role will help me grow as a ______(new career).

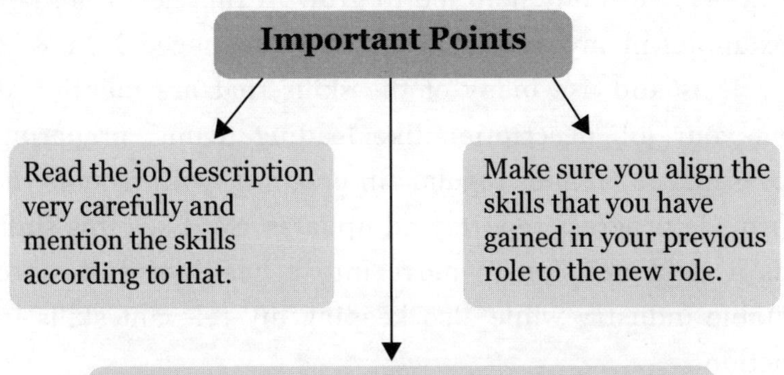

Sample Answer 3 (Experienced Professional) (Role: Generic)

I want to change my career path for better opportunities and growth. I am confident that my skills and experience will transfer well into this career. For example, I read that communication and leadership skills were mentioned in the job description a couple of times. That's my core strength. I am really excited to make this switch and follow my passion.

Sample Answer 4 (Experienced Professional) (Role: Generic)

My current industry is facing a lot of challenges and is struggling a lot. Moreover, as my current industry has many overlaps with ABC industry (mention the industry where you want to switch now) I will be able to contribute quickly. The skills that I have developed in my previous role will certainly help me to grow in this new role. For example, in my current role I have managed X, Y & Z projects and use many of the skills that are mentioned on your job description like leading teams, preparing presentations and regular interaction with clients to provide progress reports and updates. So, I see this shift as a right decision to move into a healthier and more stable industry while also keeping my relevant skills in action.

4.3.5 Why are you changing your job so soon?

NOTE: Always remember frequently changing jobs can be a red flag and might decrease your chances of getting hired. So it's important that you handle this question carefully.

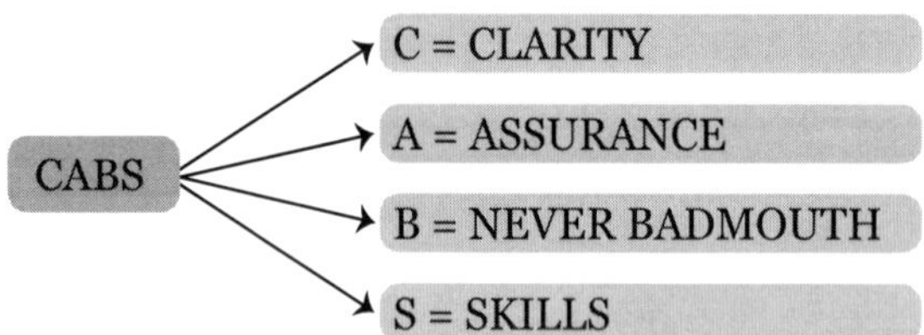

Follow my formula CABS

- Portray **Clarity** of mind
- **Assure** that you will stick with the company in long run
- **Never Badmouth** previous Employers

- Talk about how your **Skills** will help them meet the company goals.

Sample Answer 1

I joined ABC company as a X (mention your industry), but I realized that my immense skills are in Y (mention the industry that you want to join) . In your company, I have seen the job for the position of Y with great work culture and work-life balance which attracted me to apply for this role.

Sample Answer 2

Although my current job is giving me the opportunity, I want to challenge myself with new harder opportunities, that's why I decided to change my job. I love to take on challenges and learn from them to see myself as a responsible person in a reputed organization. By utilizing the opportunities offered by the organization, I want to develop myself professionally and break my own limits.

Sample Answer 3

When I took the job, I was eager for employment and had not evaluated whether the position was a good fit for me or not. Eventually, I realized the environment did not match my preferred working style. Now that I realize how important a collaborative environment is to me, I take more time to research companies before applying." I have read the job description and your company's X and Y projects are something that I would love to be part of. I know I have the right skill set to help you get the upcoming projects running.

4.3.6 Are you willing to relocate?

What does the interviewer want to know?

- Are you an adaptable person?
- If the company requires you to shift/ relocate, what will be your decision?

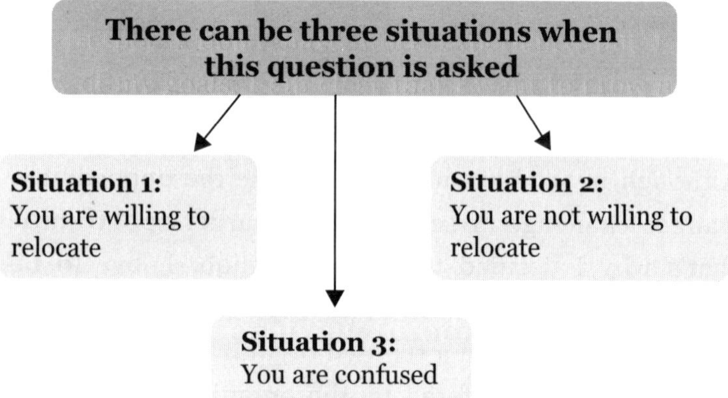

Here are the sample answers depending upon these three situations:

Situation 1 (If you are willing to relocate)

I am definitely willing to relocate to be part of this company and the team. I am always open to explore new career opportunities.

Situation 2 (If you are not willing to relocate)

This is a great opportunity for my career and would love to be a part of the team here. I have a deep connection to this area and feel it is the ideal place for me to continue growing professionally, especially with your company.

Situation 3 (If you are confused)

I very much enjoy this area and would love to continue my career here, but this position is a great opportunity for my career and if relocating is a part of it, I would definitely consider the option depending upon the circumstances.

4.3.7 Would You Consider Taking Less Pay Than You Made in Your Last Job?

Sample Answer 1

Ma'am with all due respect I really need to know more about my responsibilities and your whole package before I give an exact answer to this question. After I know about the perks and bonuses that are given to the employees for this position and role, I will be able to decide with clarity.

Sample Answer 2

Opportunity is valuable to me. I am always willing to look at the bigger picture. However, I would like to be paid according to what I bring to the position, but I am certainly flexible to ensure we are in alignment for the same.

4.4 SECTION 4: CONFIDENCE

1. How did you hear about this position?
2. What do you know about our company?
3. Why should we hire you?

4. Why did you leave your previous company?
5. Why were you fired from your previous job?
6. What other companies are you interviewing with?

4.4.1 How did you hear about this position?

What does the interviewer want to know?

- The job source from which you heard about the position.
- What aspects drew you to this position?

Common Mistakes

- **Not being prepared** – For example by saying "I don't remember or I am unsure about the source."
- **Randomly saying that you saw it online** – Avoid lying about it. If you did not see the job opening on the job board, avoid saying that you saw it on the job board. Be truthful and honest.
- **Avoid speaking out things which might make it sound like you apply to every job you come across** - This will only show your desperation as a job seeker who lacks passion and simply wants to get an offer letter.

Approach to answer this question

- Keep your answer simple and short
- Show energy and excitement
- Mention the resource if you remember
- Mention that you have researched about the company

- Give specific reasons why you were looking for this position

Resources from where you can possibly know about the job opening can be:

- From an employee
- From an online Job Posting
- From a company's website
- From a recruiter
- From an article/ press release/ newspaper

Sample Answer 1 (from an employee)

I have a friend in this company who told me about the opening for this position. I was pretty excited as I knew my skills and educational background matches with the job description. So, I wanted to apply and learn more about the opportunity.

Sample Answer 2 (From an online job posting)

I found the job posting for this position on __________ (for example: Facebook, Naukri.com, Monster.com, LinkedIn) while searching for an "X" position. I reviewed the job description and it seemed like a great potential fit.

Sample Answer 3 (From a company's website)

I was visiting your company's website and saw that there is an opening for an "X" position. I was pretty glad as I have been really looking forward to this opportunity.

Sample Answer 4 (From a recruiter)

I was contacted by a recruiter who put me in touch with your company. I was eagerly waiting for a job opening at your company for an "X" position. As I know, I have the right skill set that can help me, as well as the company to grow.

Sample Answer 5 (From an article/ press release/ newspaper)

I read about this position in _________. I got really excited and did further research on your company via your website. After reading the job description I decided to apply as I knew I can be a great fit for this role if I am chosen to contribute.

4.4.2 What do you know about our company?

What does the interviewer want to know?

- Have you researched about the company before applying?

Common Mistakes

- **Not reading about the company's background**
- **Giving compliments that are not true** – (for example: if you tell a start-up or a small business company that they are the biggest names you know in the industry, you will sound authentic)

Things you should read on the company's website:

1. What is their revenue model?
2. How is their customer service?
3. Who are their typical clients / customers?
4. Approx. How many employees do they have?
5. When was the company founded?
6. Who are their biggest competitors?
7. What are the recent projects they are working on?
8. Anything that makes them stand out?

Resources to research about the company

- Company's website
- Social Media – Facebook, Twitter, Instagram and LinkedIn

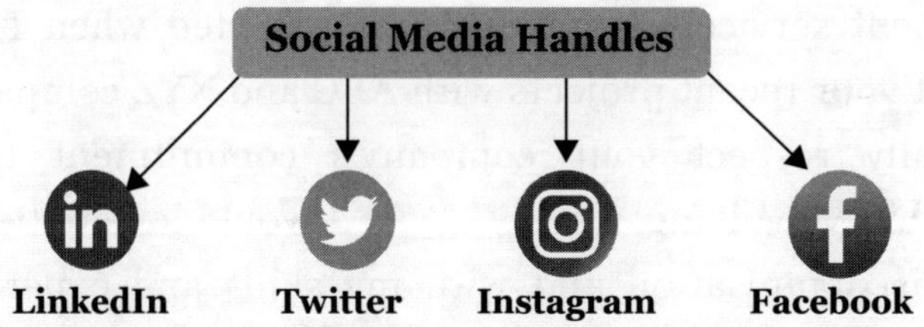

- Google News for company's name

Approach to answer this question

- Conduct a thorough research about the company to answer this question confidently.
- Pick two or three specific facts about the company.
- Make it about the company and not yourself.

Sample Answer 1 (Applying to an MNC)

I know you are one of the biggest providers of ______ and you were founded in ______. I feel a real connection to the mission and values of this company and I am so impressed by how much it has grown over the last several years. I also read that you have _____ employees worldwide. Your company is one of the top names in the industry, which is why I was really excited when I read about the job opportunity for "X" position. It would be great if I am chosen to contribute to this prestigious company.

Sample Answer 2 (Applying to a Mid-size company)

I know that this company was founded in _______ by ______ . Since then, this company has been providing excellent services. It got me really excited when I read about your recent projects with ABC and XYZ companies. I really respect your company's commitment to be constantly evolving. As a _______ I would love to be part of this organisation and with my skills and experience in the "Y" industry for ____ years. I strongly believe I can add true value to this company if I am chosen to contribute.

Sample Answer 3 (Applying to a Start – up)

I strongly believe that it's a great learning experience when you work with a start-up. So when I heard about the job opening at your company I was really keen to apply. I know this company has been recently formed in _____ year with _____ number of employees on board. With your upcoming project with ABC I can be of great help as I have the right skill set that will help you to get the project running. What I love the most about this company is that you have a vision to see a problem and think of an innovative idea to address it. It was great to know that this company also received an award for ______ recently.

4.4.3 Why should we hire you?

What does the interviewer want to know?

- Do you have the right skill set as per the job description?
- Are you a problem solver?
- Will you stick with the company in the long run?

Approach to answer this question

- Think of skills or points that will help you stand out. Show how you are unique.
- Show a connection between your skills and the company's requirements.
- Then, create a precise script that includes all the relevant topics, highlighting your skills, experience, and expertise.
- Show your deep interest in the job you are applying for.

Important Tip

To understand the company's requirements it's essential that you read the job description thoroughly. Understand their business model, revenue model, upcoming projects and most importantly what problems they are trying to solve.

Do a deep research about the company. The best way to do this is to visit the company's website, follow their social media handles and read any relevant news articles that can provide you with a deeper insight of what exactly the company is looking for in its employees.

Sample Answer 1 (Experienced professionals) (Role: Generic)

Before applying for the interview I did a thorough research about your company. As I know you are looking for someone who has experience in the "X" industry I truly believe I can bring a lot to the table. Apart from that, I also have good communication skills which is another requirement to deal with clients on a daily basis. Because of these reasons I strongly believe that I am a great fit for the job.

Sample Answer 2 (Experienced professionals) (Role: Teacher)

I possess a thorough understanding of your school's mission and feel that I will be able to contribute immensely. My focus is always on how to help students meet their academic goals. My 5 years of teaching experience has taught me to understand the dynamic needs of my students. I am sure that my past experience and mentoring skills will add a lot of value if I am chosen to contribute.

Sample Answer 3 (Experienced professionals) (Role: HR coordinator)

I know as per your job description that you are looking for someone who has experience in maintaining agendas and assisting payrolls. My 5 years of experience in XY Company has trained me well to take care of any assigned clerical and administrative work. Above that, I am also trained well in coordinating training sessions, helping with interviews and evaluating job applications. I truly believe with all this experience I am a great fit for this job.

Sample Answer 4 (Experienced professionals (Role: soft engineer)

As per the job description I have good knowledge of this industry. With 7 years of experience in software development I am well trained in meeting deadlines. I also have good communication and problem solving skills that will help in greater customer satisfaction. I strongly believe that I will be able to contribute to your upcoming projects with ABC and XYZ companies, right from day one.

Sample Answer 5 (Freshers) (If you have been good in academics)

I believe I am skilled at communication skills. I was an excellent orator in college. I feel proud to mention that I have always scored the highest in computer science. The internships that I have done have trained me well to meet the deadlines. My excellent academic record is a proof of my sincerity and hardworking nature. Although I don't have work experience and a lot of work knowledge, I think by putting significant efforts, I shall surely learn. I can assure you that I will be an asset to this company if I am chosen to contribute.

Sample Answer 6 (Freshers) (If you were an average student)

In your job description I noticed that you are looking for someone who has good knowledge about "X" . It has always been my passion to learn new things related to "X". I have also done a few freelance projects that have given me exposure in the "X" field. Although I don't have much experience to demonstrate my skills, with dedication and hard work I assure you that I will soon become a productive member of your team.

Sample Answer 7 (Freshers) (If you were active in college events)

I have always been very active in my College. Right from organizing college events such as debate competitions and College fests I have been appreciated for my management skills. To ensure everything runs smoothly I am a planned person who believes in proper communication. My 3 years of active participation has made me a really good team player who can work in any environment. As this job requires me to do ______ and _____ I truly believe I have that right skill set. As I am a fresher I don't have much work experience but I know with dedication and hard work I will soon become a productive member of your team.

Scan below to watch detailed video on answering "Why should we hire you?"

4.4.4 Why did you leave your previous company?

What does the interviewer want to know?

- Honest Reason and an explanation for leaving the job.
- Do you have clarity of your goals?

Approach to answer this question:

- Never bad mouth your previous company, coworkers or your boss.
- Always start your answer by focusing on what experience you have gained from your previous company.

Sample Answer 1 (When you are moving for a promotion)

I will always be grateful to ABC company (mention the name of your previous company here). My 5 years of experience in the "X" industry has taught me how to define problems, conduct and narrow down research, finding and analysing solutions and making best decisions for the team. Being an integral part of the team and handling big clients with 80% customer satisfaction, I strongly believe that it is time to be promoted to a senior position. I spoke regarding the same with my supervisor but currently there was no room to promote me.

Sample Answer 2 (When you are moving for a higher pay)

My 3 years of experience in the previous company has taught me how to push myself beyond limits. I have always been a top performer and I have introduced innovative ideas such as _____ and _____ in my previous role. I believe I am fully prepared to join a company that values my skills and the extra work that I put in. As much as I respect my seniors' appreciation that I have always received while I worked with ABC (name of previous company) , the financial reward equally motivates me to keep going.

Sample Answer 3 (When you are moving because you don't like the job)

I left my last job because I realised that my skills and aspirations were not aligned with the position. I joined ABC company as a fresh graduate and I have learnt a lot in the 3 years of working with them. The company was great but the position did not offer enough challenges to fully utilise my skills and abilities. I have read about the work culture and value system of your company. The job description blends well with my long-term career goals. Given my experience in _____ from the previous role, I am optimistic about adding immense value to this position from day one.

Sample Answer 4 (When you relocated to a different city)

I had to quit because I moved from ______ . I will always appreciate the encouragement, mentorship and 3 years of valuable experience that I gained while working with XYZ company. I am excited to be here and add value to your company if I am chosen to contribute.

Sample Answer 5 (When you decided to make a shift in your career)

I have always enjoyed my job as a content creator but my favourite part has always been handling social media accounts, reaching customers and building brand awareness. For these reasons, I decided to make a shift in my career and work as a digital marketer. To up-skill my knowledge I also completed a certification course from Coursera. I am well aware that it will be like starting my career from the beginning and hitting a restart button but I truly believe I have the talent to explore further as a digital marketer.

4.4.5 Why were you fired from your previous job?

If you say you were fired from your last job, there's a small risk that an interviewer will judge you.

On the other hand, if you lie, that's also a risk and could end the interview process when they do a background check.

In my experience as an Interview Coach, the risk of lying is greater.

So if you were fired, the best approach is to be honest about why you are no longer in that former position, accept responsibility, and then explain what you have learnt from your mistake and ensure it never happens again.

What does the interviewer want to know?

- Why were you fired?
- What have you learnt from your experience?

Approach to answer this question

- Be upfront and explain the grounds of removal from the job.
- Don't appear uncomfortable.
- Don't lie. Explain the reason and focus on what you have learnt.
- Ensure the employer that it won't be repeated again and will not affect your performance in case you are hired.

Sample Answer 1

Fired because of lack of performance

I was let go from my past position because I wasn't able to meet the sales goals consistently. On the other hand I have always been appreciated for my networking. I was hired by the company as a fresh graduate because of my excellent academic records. Whereas they usually hire people with sales experience. Unfortunately, I was let go for performance issues before I had a chance to really get comfortable in the role. The skills that I have learned like – effective communication, great listening skills and coming to work with great energy, will serve me well if I am given a chance to contribute here. We can add here that - After I was fired I spent time and effort to get better at my work, and before applying for this job, I have honed my skills to the best of my current ability.

Sample Answer 2

Fired because of misconduct

The company had a zero-tolerance policy of not using cell phones during working hours. I was going through some serious family issues, so it was unavoidable to not check my phone. The matter was soon reported to manager and he told me because they have lot of confidential data the rules are strict and clear for everyone. For this reason I was let go. I certainly regret not bringing this up and discussing it openly with my manager. I am pretty sure if I would have honestly communicated the issue to him he would have helped me. From this experience I have realised how important it is to keep your seniors in loop and communicate with them if there is an issue. I understand that company policies exists for a reason and I ensure you that no such problem will arise in the future.

4.4.6 What other companies are you interviewing with?

- Start by stating where you have applied to
- Vaguely mention how many interviews you may have coming up if any
- Firmly state why this role in particular is exactly what you want
- Finish by adding which of your skills makes you the perfect candidate

Sample Answer 1

I have a couple of interviews coming up soon with X,Y,Z companies for ABC positions. But I can tell you that, based on what I know, this position has exactly what I'm looking for in my next role.

Sample Answer 2

I have three other interviews scheduled with other companies. I chose this company as my primary choice because it has a supportive, diverse company culture, and I believe I'm a good match for it.

4.5 SECTION 5: JOB-COMPETENCE

1. Describe yourself in one word.
2. What would your previous boss say about you?
3. How do you respond to interruptions when you are working on critical projects?
4. What is your biggest achievement?

5. How did you learn and develop your professional skills?
6. How much training do you think you'll need to become a productive employee?

4.5.1 Describe yourself in one word.

Keep this point in mind: -

- Just using big words of vocabulary without any proof of excellence is of no good use to the interviewer. Rather, identify your key skills and strengths and find a word that fits your personality and the job role.

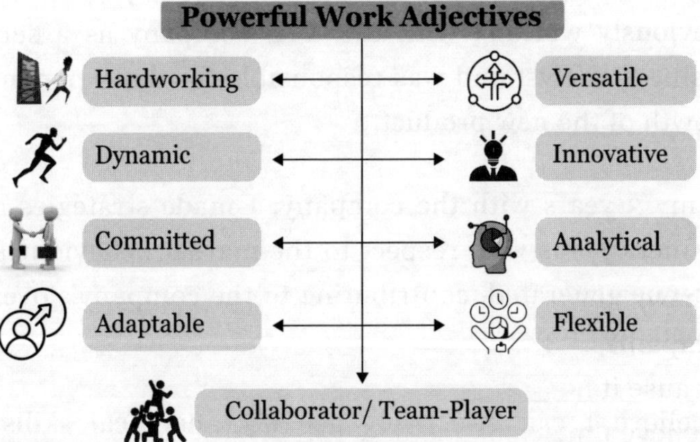

Sample Answer 1 (Versatile)

I'm a versatile person with the ability to deliver results in a constantly changing scenario. I can easily adapt to new plans, strategize and execute the tasks seamlessly.

In my experience as a project manager, I have led teams in agile circumstances and met the organizational goals for the last 2 years.

Sample Answer 2 (Dynamic)

I think the one word that describes me the best is dynamic. In my 5 years of work experience, I have been caught off-guard in many situations where the strategies and goals changed in a blink.

I have delivered well in environments where nothing was certain. I can adapt to any changes in the organization and will always perform well.

Sample Answer 3 (Analytical)

The word that best describes me is analytical. I was previously working with the XYZ company as a senior business analyst and was responsible for the exponential growth of the new product.

In my 3 years with the company, I made strategies and business plans with respect to the market behaviour and revenue generated, contributing to the company's overall growth by 11.3%.

I believe I can effectively use my analytical skills to identify the measures that must be taken to ensure the growth of the organization.

Sample Answer 4 (Innovative)

I'm very innovative and love finding new things that can intrigue me. Professionally speaking, I like to experiment with new ways to do things and achieve the desired results within the set time frame.

In my previous role, I worked on the development of an ABC application and it was a huge success in the market, standing out with its distinctive features.

Sample Answer 5 (Team Player)

I would describe myself as a team player. I'm very comfortable working with people and understand the dynamics of working in a group. My previous role required me to work directly with 10 of my colleagues and involved frequent inter-team interaction.

I have always been able to perform well and resolve any hiccups the team faces.

4.5.2 What would your previous boss say about you?

What does the interviewer want to know?

- Do you have the ability to build strong and meaningful professional relationships?
- Any impressive skills that would help the company to grow?

Approach to answer this question

- Cite an example of when you received a recognition, award, appraisal or promotion.
- Talk about at least one specific personality trait that makes you stand out. (Trait should be aligned with the job description)

Sample Answer 1

My previous boss always appreciated me for my planning skills. He often relied on me for complicated tasks, believing that I would be of full assistance to him. I in fact remember how one time I was specially appreciated in a team meeting for chalking out a plan to finish two projects that were overlapping with each other to meet the deadlines.

Sample Answer 2

Honestly, she would say I am very warm and friendly. She always praised me for being a patient listener. My fellow employees often laugh at how I am every customer's favorite employee. I truly believe that's a great skill that adds to positive customer feedback.

Sample Answer 3

My previous boss would describe me as an organized person. For instance, I helped my entire team to implement a new system that keeps a track of every important document. It also helped our department to keep files in order. She once told me that I am always responsive and coming up with new ideas to solve complicated problems.

Sample Answer 4

My previous employer would describe me as an innovative and creative person. She always appreciated me for my insightful ideas to get the projects running. During my last performance review, I received an award for the best leadership skills. I think he feels this way because I am, even in my personal life, always enthusiastic and an initiator.

Sample Answer 5

I believe he would describe me as good with conflict management. I have the skills to mediate the matter and help people to calm down. I have always been told by my fellow employees that I have a positive attitude. I believe that it has a lot to do with my personal nature as I truly believe that it's essential to be considerate and try to let go of things rather than blowing the matter out of proportion. It helps us to stay focused and not waste our energy on unproductive things.

4.5.3 How do you respond to interruptions when you are working on critical projects?

What does the interviewer want to know?

- How do you handle difficult situations?
- How adaptive are you?
- Do you lose your focus easily?

Approach to answer this question:

- Always show that you are flexible, adaptive and can handle difficult situations
- Show that you are patient and your prime focus is to deliver good results

Sample Answer 1 (Role: Generic) (Fresher)

Interruptions can cause delay in meeting deadlines if we lose our focus. However, it can also always help us to improve and learn more. I have always paid attention to the areas that need improvement. I believe the reason my recent project was given so much appreciation was because of my college faculty. Two best professors of my college were guiding me. There were a lot of interruptions I faced before my draft was finally accepted but I would say that it was a learning experience for me. It taught me that patience is the key to face interruptions and one should only focus on producing the best results.

Sample Answer 2 (Role: Generic) (Experienced Candidate)

I have a solution-based approach. Once while working on a critical project, the client kept on calling me to ask about the progress of the project after every 2-3 days. In order to mitigate the interruptions, I assigned a trusted assistant to handle the client's calls. I briefed the assistant with all the intricacies of the project so he had all the necessary information available with him to ensure that the clients questions were answered. This helped me to focus on the project and deliver the best.

4.5.4 What is your biggest achievement?

What does the interviewer want to know?

- The kinds of benefits the company will gain by employing you

Approach to answer this question

- Mention relevant and recent achievements.
- Explain what you accomplished and why was it important
- Highlight the benefits of your achievement to the employer

Examples of common achievements that you can mention in an Interview

1. Innovative changes (A time when you implemented a solution to make your company more efficient and productive)
2. Revenue Increase
3. Improved Customer's experience
4. Took a lead on a project and delivered positive outcome
5. Co-Curricular activities
6. Certification Courses
7. Mentoring a co-worker or fellow student.

Sample Answer 1 (Fresher)

My biggest professional achievement is that while I was completing my graduation I did a part time job as YZX (for e.g. customer executive) . To be honest, it was challenging because I had to also focus on my grades but simultaneously I was passionate about learning new things. I am quite grateful as now I have good experience before I can take on this job full time. I have realized that prioritizing time and staying focused are keys to success.

Sample Answer 2 (Experienced Professional)

Role: HR Administrator

My biggest professional achievement has been implementing a team filing system. I noticed my team members often faced difficulty in locating specific files which reduced productivity, particularly during busy periods. So this new system that I created, streamlined everything and reduced the time spent on looking for required files by several hours.

Sample Answer 3 (Experienced Professional)

Role: Teacher

I feel so happy when I think of the fact that I have contributed to improving the grades of so many students by always being available to them. As teachers we are responsible to not only impart education but also to encourage students so that they remain focused. I would love to mention that when it was brought to my notice that students are feeling demotivated before the exams I personally spoke to the principal and took her approval on arranging a seminar. The core motto of the seminar was to motivate students so that they don't feel nervous. I truly believe that apart from academic help, helping students emotionally is equally important. Every student was extremely thankful for this initiative taken by the school.

Sample Answer 4 (Experienced Professional)

Role: Generic

My biggest achievement is when I was working with ABC company I worked on XYZ project. The person who was leading the project had to resign from the job due to some personal issues. I had to fill in for him and take the lead. I saw this coming as a great opportunity rather than a challenge. I really delivered an exceptional presentation, outlining all the important aspects of the project. Not only my teammates were happy but my boss gave me a glowing performance review.

4.5.5 How did you learn and develop your professional skills?

What does the interviewer want to know?

- ➷ The interviewer wants you to discuss your skills, education, and training as professional experiences.

Approach to answer this question:

- ➷ Focus on briefly telling the interviewer how did you acquire the skills
- ➷ Only talk about the relevant skills that matches with the job description
- ➷ Talk about how your education/ professional experience will help you to meet the company needs.

Sample Answer 1 (Role Generic) (Fresher)

I was always passionate about becoming ______ (mention your role here) (For example: Engineer) .

I knew to get placed well in my career I had to develop communication skills, analytical skills and problem-solving skills. For this my focus was always to study and understand the concepts in depth. I also did X and Y courses from Coursera to enhance my communication skills. I truly believe my focus and determination towards my career has contributed in helping me acquire all the relevant skills that will help me to fit in this role.

Sample Answer 2 (Role Generic) (Experienced Candidate)

As an experienced ______ (mention your role here) I was always keen to get my hands on learning and acquiring new skills that will help me to advance in my professional career. For this I actively participated in team events and also completed the XYZ training programme. All of this has helped me to grow in my professional career. I also read that presentation and communication skills were mentioned in the job description. My previous experience has trained me well to acquire these two core skills that will certainly help me to meet the company requirements.

4.5.6 How much training do you think you'll need to become a productive employee?

Similar interview questions:

- How quickly do you think you will come up to speed in this role?
- Do you think you will need lots of supervision as you start out in this role?

Points to keep in mind:

- Tailor your answer according to the employer's expectations.
- In order to know this, read the job description really well and dig deeper by researching about the company. You can do this by reading the company's website.

Sample Answer 1 (Experienced Candidates)

Given my background and X years of experience, I'm confident that I will be productive immediately. I will need time to familiarize myself with your internal systems, however I am sure it will not take much time for me to get hold of the work here. I understand your need to fill this role as quickly as possible and I can assure you that I will be productive from day one.

Sample Answer 2 (Freshers)

My education and internship experience has prepared me well for this role. I am exceptionally good at presentation and communication skills, which is why I feel I will be a valuable asset to the company from day one. Moreover, I understand that you also provide internal training for new hires related to the role and your company. Given this training, combined with my education and skills, I'm confident that I will come up to speed quickly in this role.

4.6 SECTION 6: LEVEL OF COMMITMENT

1. How do you handle stress?
2. Why do you want to work with us?

3. Are you applying to other companies as well?
4. Why do you want this job?
5. Why are you interviewing for this company when you already have a job offer?
6. What are your future plans?

4.6.1 How do you handle stress or pressure?

What does the interviewer want to know?

- Does stress affect your performance?
- A real life experience, how you handled the situation and what was the outcome.

Approach to answer this question

Show the employer how you manage stress. That way, the interviewer can build up a clear picture of how well you adapt to stressful situations. For example, describe a time when you were given a difficult task or multiple assignments and how you rose to the occasion.

Focus on success. When you respond, share examples of how you succeeded despite being in a stressful situation, or of how you solved the problem to resolve the issue that caused stress.

Use The "STAR METHOD" To Answer This Question

S = SITUATION
T = TASK
A = ACTION
R = RESULT

Sample Answer 1 (Fresher)

I actually work better under pressure, and I've found that I enjoy working in a challenging environment. For example, I once had three large projects due in the same week, and that was a lot of pressure. However, because I created a task sheet that detailed how I would break down each project into small assignments, I managed to complete all three projects ahead of time and avoided unnecessary stress.

Sample Answer 2 (Fresher)

I've found that a healthy amount of stress motivates me to stay on track and work as efficiently and effectively as possible. As I was the captain of the basketball team, I have often juggled stressful situations quite well. Once a very important player had to quit a day before the match because of an unavoidable medical emergency. The morale of the entire team was shaken. I made sure to encourage the substitute player and showed full confidence in him. His performance was phenomenal and we won the college tournament.

Sample Answer 3 (Experienced Candidate) (Role: Management)

As someone who has spent the past five years in a management role, I understand that stressful situations are just a part of the job. To overcome such situations, instead of panicking I outline my schedule and map out my tasks. Then I prioritize what is most important. This way I am always able to meet the deadlines and avoid unnecessary stress.

For example, my project, for which I won an XYZ award, was assigned to me only days before the due date. I used the pressure of that deadline to harness my knowledge and focus.

Sample Answer 4 (Experienced Candidate)

A little bit of stress can actually be a motivator for me. I use the pressure to stay focused on my tasks and produce work more efficiently. I believe with proper communication and team work stressful deadlines can easily be handled. My approach to handle stress is always to remain calm and focus on completing the most important tasks first.

4.6.2 Why do you want to work with us?

What does the interviewer want to know?

- Have you researched the company?
- Do your long-term goals align with the company?
- How can you help the company succeed?

Tip – Do extensive research about the company and its industry.

Things you should know about the company:

- Has it recently changed its products or services?
- What competitive pressures is it facing?
- What skills do you have to get the projects running?

Approach to answer this question

- Align your knowledge and skills to the company needs.
- Be specific and short while answering this question.

Sample Answer 1 (Experienced Professionals)

When I saw that there was a job opening at your company, I was really excited to apply for it. I have seen your work in the XYZ project and I must say it was phenomenal. It was truly inspiring and since then I have been waiting for a job opportunity here. Moreover, I also read about your upcoming project with ABC company. I have 7 years of experience in ____ and the right skill set that has prepared me for this role.

Note:

This is a perfect response as it demonstrates the candidate's knowledge of the company. It shows that he/she is aware of their projects and has researched about what the company is looking for in its new hiring. The candidate then relates it to his previous experience that can help the company to grow.

Sample Answer 2 (Experienced Professionals)

It would be great to work with your company. Before applying I did some research on the company and I believe that the company's ABC products and its future projections are very promising. I know I have the right skills that can help you to get the upcoming projects running.

Sample Answer 3 (Fresh Graduates)

I would be proud to work for a company like yours with such a long history of leadership in the industry. I strongly believe this is the right place where my skills and backgrounds fit perfectly and will be put to optimum use.

Sample Answer 4 (Fresh Graduates)

I have always looked towards organizations like yours to kickstart my career.

As a fresher I don't have work experience but I have clarity of my goals. I am clear that I want to grow myself as _____ (for e.g., an advocate) in your ____ (for e.g., civil law) department. I have always been the top performer in my college. I can assure you that I will work with sincerity and bring a noteworthy contribution to this company.

4.6.3 Are you applying to other companies as well?

What does the interviewer want to know?

- Are you serious and passionate about this company?
- Do you already have an offer in your hand?

Approach to answer this question

- Be honest if you have applied for other companies
- Show the reason you have interviewed for other companies is because you want to explore what is best suited for your career growth
- Your answer should reflect honesty, passion for the company you are interviewing for. The interviewer should not feel that his time is not being respected.

Sample Answers if you have applied for other companies

Sample Answer 1 (Role: Generic) (Freshers + Experienced Candidates)

Yes. I have submitted my applications in some of the best companies like [....].

Above all, my priority and hope is that I will be able to land a job at your company.

Sample Answer 2 (Role: Generic) (Freshers + Experienced Candidates)

I do have a couple of interviews coming up soon with X,Y & Z companies for ABC positions. But I can tell you that, based on what I know, this position has exactly what I'm looking for in my next role.

Sample Answer 3 (Role: Generic) (Freshers + Experienced Candidates)

I have three other interviews scheduled with other companies. I chose this company as my primary choice because it has a supportive, diverse company culture, and I believe I'm a good match for it.

Sample Answer if haven't applied for any other company (Role: Generic) (Freshers + Experienced Candidates)

I am not currently interviewing with any other companies because I wanted to focus on securing a position with your company. I'm really excited to be here. I'm hoping to use my skills to help the company grow, and your company's position seems to offer the best opportunity to meet my goals.

4.6.4 Why do you want this job?

Interviewing for MNC

I have admired this company's successful strategies and mission for years. Your emphasis on creating a relationship between your company and the surrounding community have brought you success everywhere you have opened an office. These are values I greatly admire.

Interviewing for Start-ups

I understand that this is a company on the rise. As I've read on your website and in various press releases, you're planning to launch several new products in the coming months. I want to be a part of this business as it grows, and I know that I can bring my experience in X and Y to facilitate your company in rolling out these products.

4.6.5 Why are you interviewing for this company when you already have a job offer?

NOTE:-

From this question the interviewer is basically wanting to know that if you already have an offer why haven't you accepted it?

You can turn this question in your favour as it shows you are eligible and other companies (might be their competitor) have already recognised your talent which itself becomes a proof of your suitability for the job.

SAMPLE ANSWER (Fresher + Experienced Candidate)

I have an offer in hand but the reason I am interviewing for this company is because I want to explore what's best for me. I want to work for a company where my skills and experience will be put to optimum use. After reading the job description for this company, I was really excited as I knew I have the right skill set that will help me to meet the company needs.

4.6.6 What are your future plans?

NOTE: When talking about future goals, show that you are ambitious and career oriented, but without giving the impression that this job is only a stepping stone. Rather your answer should reflect that you see your future with the company.

OPTION 1 (COMMUNICATE FLEXIBILITY)

I am very open to whatever opportunities the future may hold, especially within this company. I pride myself in being flexible and adaptable. I applied for this job because I strongly believe it is a perfect fit for my interests and skill set.

OPTION 2 (SHOW MOTIVATION)

In five years, I hope to be on a career path that will lead to a supervisory position in your company. I also plan to finish my online certification course in XY within two years.

OPTION 3 (ADD VALUE)

My future plans include securing a position as a social media strategist. I know the company is interested in reaching a younger clientele, and I have the skills to help with the social media part of the new ad campaign, if hired for the advertising assistant job that is available.

4.7 SECTION 7: LEADERSHIP SKILLS

1. Describe a time when you had to take charge of a situation?
2. How do you handle tough decisions?
3. What strategies do you use to motivate your team?
4. What have been your most successful leadership experiences and why?
5. How do you ensure everyone on the team is working towards the same goal?
6. What do you think are the most important qualities of an effective leader?

Correct Approach to handle leadership questions:-

Let's use the "STAR" Technique to help you answer leadership interview questions thoroughly.

Here's how to use the STAR approach:

- **S = Situation:** Here, you describe a situation where you exhibited quality leadership.
- **T = Task:** Identify the tasks you completed that show your leadership skills.
- **A = Action:** Outline the specific actions you took to achieve the goals you set.

- **R = Result:** Talk about the positive outcome you have achieved

Using the STAR strategy, you can demonstrate to the interviewer how you have displayed your leadership skills.

4.7.1 Describe a time when you had to take charge of a situation?

What does the interviewer want to know?

- Interviewer wants to access your problem solving skills
- He wants to test your patience level
- He wants to see if you are a leader and a performer

Sample Answer 1

Job Role: Customer Service Representative

Once I had to take charge of a situation while working in my previous role as a Customer Service Representative. The situation arose when I received a call from a customer who was extremely frustrated and needed assistance. I immediately acted upon the situation to provide an effective solution to his problem. I stayed calm and composed and took the time to listen to his concerns, acknowledge their feelings and empathize with the experience they had gone through. I then offered them a few solutions and provided them with step-by-step instructions on how they could resolve the issue. In the end, the customer was satisfied with my solution and thanked me for my help. It was a great feeling knowing that I had taken charge of the situation and been able to provide help and resolution for the customer to their satisfaction.

Note: This sample answer can be used for all those job roles where employees have to interact with customers.

Sample Answer 2

Job Role: Data Analyst

In my previous company, I was closely working and contributing on the launch of their new product and needed to ensure their data was up-to-date and structured properly for the launch. I identified errors in the data, quickly recognized the potential for inaccurate results, and immediately took the initiative to ensure that all data was accurate before launch.

I worked closely with the development team to identify any issues and set up tests to validate the accuracy of the data. I also built SQL queries to obtain the relevant information needed for the launch. Furthermore, I provided detailed documentation after analysing the data, including suggested improvements for accuracy.

In the end, my efforts ensured that all data was accurate and up-to-date for the product launch, helping to make it a success.

Sample Answer 3

Job Role: Software Engineer

As a Software Engineer, I recently had a situation where I had to take charge in order to fix a critical software issue. The issue was related to XY.(*You can give an example of any software issue here that you are confident talking about). It had been going on for some time and the team was unable to make any progress. I took a deep dive into the code, identified the root cause, and proposed a solution. I discussed the issue with my team. After a few meetings we all could collectively find a solution. It felt great to be able to take charge and help resolve the issue quickly. Since then, I have realized how essential it is to communicate and utilize the help of my team in order to solve problems promptly.

Sample Answer (Freshers)

When I was in college. I was part of a student organization that was planning a fundraiser for charity. We had to coordinate transportation and lodging for our guests, as well as arrange food and other arrangements. Unfortunately, the person who was originally leading the project had to step down at the last minute due to other commitments. I took the initative and the entire responsibility of the event. I ensured that all of the arrangements were made in time for the event.

I organized meetings with the rest of our committee members and assigned tasks to each person according to their skills. I also monitored our progress and provided feedback where needed. Additionally, I coordinated with outside vendors and sponsors to ensure we had sufficient resources for the fundraiser. Through hard work, dedication, and determination, I was able to successfully lead the group of 80 people towards a successful event and raised funds for our chosen charity.

4.7.2 How do you handle tough decisions?

What does the interviewer want to know?

- The interviewer wants to assess how quickly you can arrive at solutions
- What is your approach to solve problems?
- Do you panic or stay calm in tough situations?
- Can you handle stress?

Sample Answer (Freshers + Experience Professionals) Role: Generic

When faced with a tough decision, I first take a step back and consider all the angles. I try to look at decisions from both a logical and emotional perspective to ensure that I am making the right decision for all parties involved. I also weigh my options by considering any potential risks or benefits that could come from a particular decision.

Moreover, I also research any and all available resources, whether that is consulting colleagues, seeking advice from a mentor or my seniors. I believe it is important to do research and uncover as much information as possible before making a decision so that I can make informed decisions.

Ultimately, my goal is to make sure that I am always able to make decisions in the best interest of myself, my team and my organization.

4.7.3 What strategies do you use to motivate your team?

Here are some of the strategies that you can use to motivate your team:-

- Setting clear and measurable goals
- Encouraging teamwork
- Maintaining proper communication
- Giving positive feedback and rewarding the team

Sample Answer (Experience Professionals) (Job Role: Generic)

To motivate my team I ensure that I always set clear and measurable goals for them. This gives them an opportunity to take ownership of their work, as they can see progress being made towards the goal. Additionally, I make sure to clearly define roles and responsibilities.. By setting clear expectations and miniating proper communication, team members know what is expected of them and are motivated to succeed. Additionally, I provide recognition for outstanding work, as well as rewards for meeting goals. Finally, I regularly communicate with my team to help ensure that everyone feels included and valued. By listening to their ideas and concerns, I am able to help foster a collaborative environment that motivates team members to work together to achieve their goals.

NOTE: There are a lot of strategies discussed in this answer. You can use any 2-3 points that resonate with your job role and the role you are applying for.

4.7.4 What have been your most successful leadership experiences and why?

How to answer this question?

- Think about your leadership experiences in the past
- Showcase your ability to be a great team player
- Outline the steps you took to achieve positive outcomes
- Discuss what have you learnt in the process

Sample Answer (Experience Professional) (Job Role: HR Executive)

As an HR Executive, one of my most successful leadership experiences was when I launched a new employee onboarding program for a large tech company. The program was designed to streamline the onboarding process, recruit the top talent, improve communication between new employees and their supervisors, and ensure that all new hires had the necessary tools and resources they needed to be successful in their new roles. Through my direction and guidance, the program was implemented seamlessly and was met with positive feedback from both new employees and managers. This experience taught me the importance of proactively managing the onboarding process, utilizing the right resources and tools, and communicating effectively with all stakeholders. Additionally, it taught me that successful leadership requires clear objectives, effective communication, and intentional planning.

Sample Answer (Job Role: Generic)

As a _______ (mention your role here), I have had several successful leadership experiences in my past professional roles. The most successful one was when I led a team of 8 members to manage _______ (talk about any of your projects here). I was tasked with managing the budget, timeline, and milestones of the project, as well as ensuring that the solution met all of the requirements.

To ensure our success, I established a clear set of goals and objectives that everyone could work towards. Furthermore, I held regular meetings with the team to discuss progress and set expectations. I also established a system of accountability by providing regular feedback and recognising those who went above and beyond.

The result of our project was that our solution was implemented on-time and within budget, while meeting the customer's requirements and expectations. This was a major success for both myself and my team, as we were able to demonstrate our leadership and problem-solving skills in a highly demanding environment.

4.7.5 How do you ensure everyone on the team is working towards the same goal?

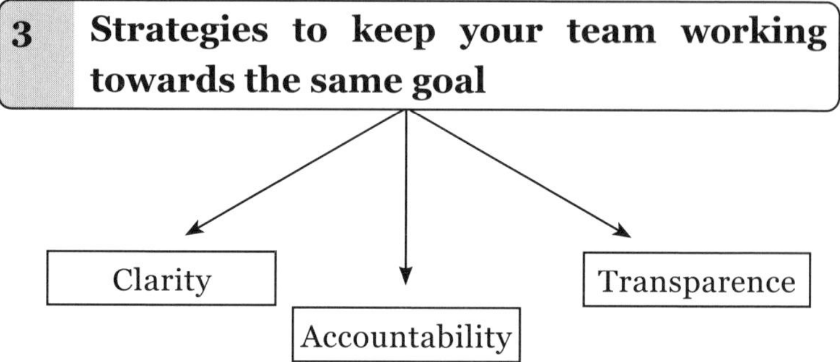

Sample Answer (Job Role: Generic)

I focus on 3 most important parameters and that is Clarity, Accountability and Transparency. I ensure everyone on the team is working towards the same goal is to create a clear and concise action plan. This plan should include measurable objectives, goals, and timelines.

Accountability plays an important role in achieving a common goal. As such, it is important to recognize individual contributions and provide feedback throughout the project.

Additionally, it would be beneficial to maintain transparency by communicating frequently with the team to discuss progress and any roadblocks. This would ensure everyone is on the same page and that the project is moving forward.

4.7.6 What do you think are the most important qualities of an effective leader?

Here are top qualities of an effective leader

- Delegation
- Self-Awareness
- Communication
- Motivator
- Empathy
- Influence

Sample Answer 1 (Delegation & Self-Awareness)

The most important qualities of an effective leader are the ability to delegate and self-awareness. Delegation is important because it allows effective leaders to take on more responsibility and to focus on the most important tasks. By delegating tasks, the leader can ensure that the projects are completed withing the stipulated time frame. Self-awareness is also essential for leaders, as it allows them to understand their strengths and weaknesses, as well as the strengths and weaknesses of their team members.

Sample Answer 2 (Communication & Motivator)

An effective leader is one who is able to Communicate their vision, goals, and expectations to their team members in a clear and concise manner. They must also be able to listen to their team member's feedback, ideas, and opinions in order to make the best decisions for their organization. An effective leader should also be able to Motivate and encourage team members through honest feedbacks and appreciation for each individual's contributions. Ultimately, an effective leader should be able to foster an environment of trust, respect, and collaboration among team members.

Sample Answer 3 (Empathy & Influence)

An effective leader should be Emphatic and have the ability to effectively Influence others. Strong communication and interpersonal skills, a willingness to take risks and make informed decisions, the capacity to motivate and inspire, and an understanding of the organization's goals and objectives are also important traits of an effective leader.

Scan below to watch a detailed video on "8 Toughest Interview Q&A"

4.8 SECTION 8: GENERAL

1. Do you like to work alone or with a team?
2. What motivates you?
3. Are you willing to work overtime?

4. Are you applying to other companies as well?
5. What was the most difficult decision you made?
6. Tell Me About Something that is not mentioned on Your Resume
7. Do you consider yourself successful?
8. Do you have any plans for further education?
9. What is the most important aspect for you in your job?
10. How Do You Define Success In Your Job?
11. How do you spend your spare time?
12. What will you do if we don't hire you?
13. Explain how your college education has prepared you for this role

4.8.1 Do you like to work alone or with a team?

Sample Answer

I can work under any management style even without any supervision. Once it is clear what my objectives are and how the company wants me to execute those objectives, I can do the job on my own as well.

Also show, that you are a team player

I also enjoy working in a team environment, and I get along well with people.

In my past work experience, I implemented a system to help organize the communication between my co - workers to enhance our productivity as a team. It helped us delegate tasks more easily, which led to completing our projects before the deadlines.

4.8.2 What motivates you?

- Mention things like Job satisfaction,
- Working towards a goal,
- Contributing to a team effort,
- Developing your skills &
- Excitement for new challenges

Sample Answer

I am a very result-oriented person. My primary motivation is to achieve the desired result. I can work alone without any supervision but I also enjoy working closely with a team. When I see myself being productive every day, it motivates me to continue. I also like to take on new challenges and go beyond my expectations to deliver good results.

4.8.3 Are you willing to work overtime?

Don't say

✖ I don't mind working overtime if I get fairly compensated!

✖ Overtime? How often do I have to do that?

Tip – Don't show your hesitation. This question is asked at times to check if you are committed and passionate about your work. So be confident and answer like this

Sample Answer (If you are okay with it)

I understand that being asked to work for an extended number of hours comes with a good reason in the first place, so I'm ok with it.

Sample Answer (If you are not okay with it)

I do want to commit to something that I won't be able to do. I have family commitments that I need to balance along with my professional life. So, I won't be able to work overtime.

4.8.4 Are you applying to other companies as well?

Sample Answer 1

Yes. I have submitted my applications in some of the best companies like [....].

Above all, my priority and hope are that I will be able to land a job at your company.

Sample Answer 2

I do have a couple of interviews coming up soon with X,Y & Z companies for ABC positions. But I can tell you that, based on what I know, this position has exactly the kinds of challenges I'm looking for in my next role.

Sample Answer 3

I have three other interviews scheduled with other companies. I chose this company as my primary choice because it has a supportive, diverse company culture, and I believe I'm a good match for it.

If you are not interviewing for any other company read the sample answer in the caption below

Sample Answer 4

I'm still pretty early in my job search. I am not currently interviewing with any other companies because I wanted to focus on securing a position with your company. I'm really excited to be here. I'm hoping to use my skills to help the company grow, and your company's position seems to offer the best opportunity to meet my goals."

4.8.5 What was the most difficult decision you made?

- Be specific
- Explain the difficult decision
- How do you handle it?
- How did it ultimately benefit your team or the company?

Sample Answer (Experienced Professional)

I was working on a team project, and my colleagues and I had to make a number of choices about how to use our limited budget. I decided to take the help of a senior and follow his strategy. Because these decisions involved group conversations, our team learned how to communicate effectively with one another, and I believe we ultimately made the best decisions for the team.

Sample Answer (Fresher)

The toughest decision I had to take was to certainly decide which career option I should opt for. I was confused between X and Y. I had passion and interest for both the industries. I chose X after a thorough research and discussions with a few seniors who are well settled in this industry, I could discover that this field has more scope in terms of growth.

4.8.6 Tell Me About Something that is Not mentioned on Your Resume

Remember your interviewer has your resume and is interested in hearing something a bit different.

Approach to answer this question

- Think of a core strength / skill set that helps you to stand out.
- Back it up with a good example.
- Convince the interviewer why he should hire you?

Some Good Skills to Say in an Interview:-

- Interpersonal skills
- Communication (verbal and written)
- Listening
- Adaptability
- Teamwork
- Analytical Skills
- Problem-Solving

- Decision-Making
- Organisation Skills
- Leadership Skills

Sample Answer 1 (Fresher)

I'm a very **detail-oriented** person. I not only focus on the results, but also believe in delivering them with perfection. In my college, my projects and assignments were always appreciated by my teachers. I have also received a certificate in _____ .

I strongly believe that I can apply my skills here and will put my best foot forward to help the company grow.

Sample Answer 2 (Experienced Candidates)

My last two employers commended my communication skills. I believe I am really good at putting across my point of view with clarity. Not only this, I always use my solid active listening skills to understand my team members. This has not only helped me to maintain transparency among all the team members but has also helped me to build great professional connections.

4.8.7 Do you consider yourself successful?

Sample Answer 1 (Experienced Candidates)

I feel successful with continuous progress. It gives me a lot of satisfaction when I work with full sincerity and the results are positive. I truly believe my hard work and dedication has never let my superiors down. So, indeed I have been successful in completing most of the tasks that have been assigned to me.

Sample Answer 2 (Freshers)

Indeed I do. During my ____ year of college, I have learned to set goals and work hard towards them. I have always been sincere and true to myself and that has enabled me to always achieve good results. And I know I will work with the same dedication if I am chosen to contribute.

4.8.8 Do you have any plans for further education?

Sample Answer 1 (Freshers)

I view learning as a lifelong process. Even though I have completed my graduation, I want to continue to learn as much as I can to become an effective _____(mention your role here) . So if that requires further training and education , I am ready and prepared to do that.

Sample Answer 2 (Experienced Candidates)

I am always open to further study if my job requires me to do that. I believe that learning is a lifelong process and it is essential to stay up to date. Especially in this competitive environment where new trends are emerging every day I would love to study further if my role requires me to do that.

4.8.9 What is the most important aspect for you in your job?

Sample Answer 1 (Experienced Candidates)

"It's important for me to be productive in my role. I am known for delivering quality results in a timely manner."

Sample Answer 2 (Fresher)

"The most important aspect of my job is being able to deliver quality results on time. This was key for me in my recent internship, where I delivered not only my core project, but also a secondary optional project."

4.8.10 How Do You Define Success In Your Job?

Sample Answer (Freshers + Experienced Candidates)

I measure my success by accomplishing goals, whether set by others or myself. Contributing meaningfully to the achievement of company objectives, while growing in my role, adding value to the team, and exceeding my manager's expectations, defines success for me at work.

4.8.11 How do you spend your spare time?

Sample Answer 1: Preparing for any exam

A lot of my spare time recently has been spent in preparing for the professional certification exam for my field. So far I have passed three out of the required tests and will be taking the fourth test next month. I hope to have my certification completed by the end of the year.

Sample Answer 2 : Reading Books

I love to read books in my spare time. I believe this habit comes with a lot of benefits especially when it comes to broadening your knowledge and improving your both verbal and written communication. The recent book I have read is ___.

Sample Answer 3: Sports

I love to keep myself fit and healthy. For this I play badminton on the weekends. This is one sport that I absolutely love. I truly believe that sports play a vital role in keeping us both physically and mentally fit.

4.8.12 What will you do if we don't hire you?

Sample Answer

If I don't get hired today, I would love to take your valuable feedback for the areas I can improve upon. As I've learned more about your company, it seems like a great fit, and I have some interesting ideas to meet the company requirements. However, if I don't make the cut, I would like to keep in touch and look for other positions in your company where I put my skills and experience to use.

4.8.13 Explain how your college education has prepared you for this role.

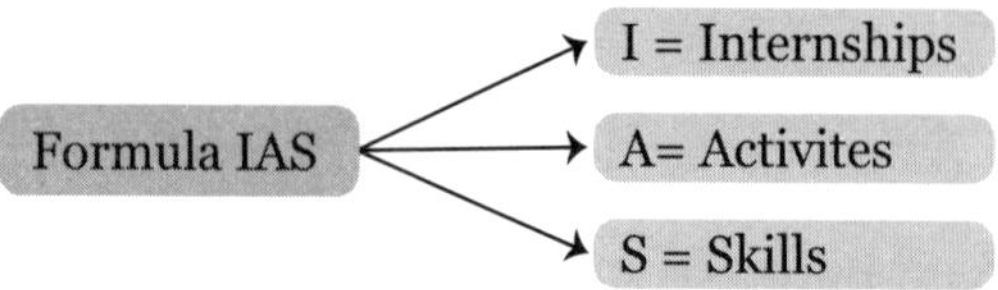

FORMULA – IAS

- Internships and Experience
- Discuss Relevant Activities
- Talk About Skills Learned

My college education has exceptionally prepared me for a smooth transition to take this job.

INTERNSHIPS

Many of my internships have given me the opportunity to experience situations first hand and taught me how to come up with the best solutions.

ACTIVITES

Project submissions have trained how to manage my time efficiently and that high-quality results take hard work.

SKILLS

Difficult subjects like X and Y have taught me exceptional critical-thinking skills and that the answers will not always be in front of my face.

CHAPTER 5

SALARY NEGOTIATION GUIDE

5.1 Why do candidates hesitate to negotiate?

- Fear of losing the job offer
- They think it's rude
- They don't know their market worth

A Good Way to Negotiate and Get Your Ideal Salary

Salary negotiation is a critical phase in the hiring process. For many candidates, it's also one of the most nerve-wracking steps. The fear of losing a job offer often holds them back from negotiating their desired salary.

However, here's the good news: **"Negotiating your salary tactfully will never cost you the job offer."** Instead, it can lead to better compensation and demonstrate your confidence and professionalism.

Let's explore the essential steps to help candidates negotiate effectively and secure their ideal salary.

1. Research Your Market Worth

Before entering into salary discussions, thorough research is essential. Use reputable salary comparison websites like:

These platforms can help you determine the average salary for your job title, location, industry, and years of experience. They also provide insights into salary trends and growth potential in your career path.

Armed with this information, you can confidently present a realistic salary range to the employer—one that aligns with the market standard and your expertise.

> **Pro Tip:** Avoid quoting an unrealistic figure, as it might make you appear out of touch with market conditions. Unrealistic expectations can lead to disqualification from the hiring process.

2. Quote a Tight Salary Range

Effective negotiation starts with knowing both your target salary and the minimum amount you're willing to accept. When presenting a salary range, ensure it's tight and based on:

- Market research
- Industry standards
- Your skills and experience

For example, if you're targeting ₹75,000 per month, avoid quoting a wide range like ₹60,000 to ₹75,000. Employers are more likely to offer the lowest figure in that range, which would be ₹60,000 in this case.

Instead, quote a tighter range, such as ₹70,000 to ₹75,000. Even if the employer offers ₹70,000, you're much closer to your ideal number.

Why It Works: A tight range communicates confidence and sets clear expectations, reducing the chances of significant downward negotiation.

3. Justify Your Salary Expectations

Providing a salary figure without justification weakens your negotiation position. Employers are more likely to consider your number if you explain how you arrived at it.

How to Justify Your Salary Expectations:

- Highlight your **skills and qualifications** that are directly relevant to the role.
- Share your **accomplishments**—quantify them whenever possible (e.g., "increased sales by 30% in 6 months" or "managed projects worth ₹1 crore").

- Emphasize what you're bringing to the table and how you can add value to the company.

By showcasing your worth, you make a compelling case for why the company should meet or exceed your expectations.

4. Avoid Creating a Deadlock

Negotiation is not a battle between you and the hiring manager—it's a collaborative process. The recruiter wants to fill the position with the right candidate as much as you want the job.

Adopting a flexible and cooperative approach can significantly improve your chances of success. Instead of making demands, frame your expectations as part of a dialogue:

- **Use phrases like:**
  - "Based on my research and experience, I believe a range of ₹70,000 to ₹75,000 is reasonable for this role."
  - "I'd like to understand if this aligns with your budget for the position."

Pro Tip: Flexibility doesn't mean compromising your worth. It means being open to a mutually beneficial solution.

5. Remember: Everything Is Negotiable

Salary isn't the only aspect you can negotiate. Many companies offer additional benefits that can enhance your overall compensation package. If the employer is unable to meet your salary expectations, consider negotiating other perks, such as:

- Relocation Expenses
- Performance Bonuses
- Additional Paid Holidays
- Transportation Allowance
- Housing or Rent Allowance
- Work-from-Home Options
- Flexible Working Hours
- Opportunities for Learning and Development
- Signing Bonuses

These benefits can significantly enhance your work-life balance and overall satisfaction, even if the base salary falls slightly short of your expectations.

Conclusion

Negotiating your salary is a skill that can be developed with preparation and practice. By researching market standards, presenting a well-justified salary range, and maintaining a flexible yet confident approach, you can turn the negotiation process in your favor.

Remember, salary negotiation isn't just about numbers—it's about showcasing your value and ensuring a win-win outcome for both you and the employer. With these strategies in mind, you're well-equipped to secure a compensation package that reflects your worth.

Now let's discuss two most important questions that you may encounter during your salary negotiation process.

Q1. What is your current CTC?

Why This Question Is Asked

The interviewer typically asks this to gauge your current salary level and use it as a basis for negotiating their offer.

Approach to Answer This Question

- Avoid disclosing your current salary unless it's absolutely necessary or mandated. Focus instead on the value you bring and the salary range they are offering.
- Politely deflect the question or redirect the conversation toward your expectations or the role's value.

3 Effective Responses to Deflect This Question

1. "I have signed an NDA (Non-Disclosure Agreement) with my current company, which restricts me from disclosing confidential information, including my salary. I hope you understand."

   This response maintains professionalism and protects your privacy.

2. "In my current role, I've significantly upskilled myself, but my salary no longer reflects my market value. Therefore, I'd prefer to focus on what this position offers rather than comparing it with my current compensation."

This positions you as a candidate focused on value and opportunity rather than just pay.

3. "The economic situation in my industry over the past few years has affected salaries, so my current pay doesn't truly reflect my expertise or market worth. I'd prefer to discuss the salary range for this position instead."

Tip: This helps you redirect the discussion toward the potential role and its compensation.

Additional Sample Answers

Sample Answer 1 (Generic, Experienced Candidate):

"Sir/Ma'am, comparing two jobs with entirely different responsibilities, base pay structures, and benefits might not be the best approach. I'd like to focus on understanding what you're offering for this role. However, if you share the salary range for this position, I can confirm if it aligns with my expectations."

Sample Answer 2 (Generic, Experienced Candidate):

"I've done my research, and based on industry data, I believe my current salary falls within the standard range. However, I'd like to learn more about the complete package and benefits for this role before we discuss specifics."

Q2. What are your salary expectations?

When This Question Is Asked

1. **Early in the interview process:** The employer is trying to gauge if your expectations align with their budget.

2. **Toward the end of the process:** They may already be inclined to select you and want to finalize the offer.

5.2 How to Respond in Different Scenarios

Scenario 1: Early in the Interview

"I would like to understand more about the role and responsibilities before discussing salary. Once we both agree that I am the right fit for the job, we can talk about compensation."

Scenario 2: Toward the End of the Interview

When the employer is likely to have decided to hire you, consider these tips:

1. **Quote a Tight Salary Range:** Research the market and propose a realistic range.

2. **Show Flexibility:** Be open to negotiation and avoid creating a deadlock.

3. **Justify Your Expectations:** Highlight your skills, experience, and certifications.

Sample Answers for Salary Expectations

Sample Answer 1:

"Based on my research, similar positions in this industry typically offer salaries in the range of ____ to ____. Considering my educational background, certifications, and the skills I bring to this role, I believe this range reflects my worth. However, I'm open to discussing the company's budget and expectations further."

Sample Answer 2:

"I am seeking compensation between ____ and ____ monthly, which I feel reflects the value I bring to the role. That said, I am flexible and would love to hear about your budget for this position, as I am very interested in contributing to your team."

5.3 Salary Negotiation Pitch

What to Do if the Employer Says, "Your Salary Expectations Are Out of Budget"

Use the CUES Formula to present your case effectively:

1. C - Certifications:

Highlight certifications or professional training that add value to your role and allow you to perform beyond basic requirements.

Example: "I have completed certifications in [specific course or tool], which enables me to handle responsibilities beyond my primary role."

2. U - Uniqueness:

Explain the unique value you bring to the table.

Example: "My ability to [specific skill or achievement] sets me apart from other candidates."

3. E - Experience/Expertise:

Reinforce your experience and expertise relevant to the position.

Example: "With [X years] of experience in [specific area], I have consistently delivered results in [specific achievements]."

4. S - Skills:

Focus on the specific skills that align with the company's goals.

Example: "My proficiency in [skills] directly addresses your team's needs for [specific challenge or project]."

Sample Negotiation Pitch

"I completely understand that the company has a budget for this role. However, I'd like you to reconsider your offer based on my qualifications and experience. Over the past [X years], I have successfully [mention specific achievements or contributions]. Additionally, I have completed [specific certifications], which equip me to take on responsibilities beyond the job description. My skills in [specific areas] will allow me to contribute to [specific projects or company goals] immediately. I am genuinely excited about this role and would feel motivated with compensation aligned to my expertise. I'd greatly appreciate it if you could take another look at the offer."

This approach balances professionalism and assertiveness, ensuring that you present yourself as a valuable asset worth the investment.

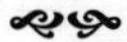

NOTES

CHAPTER 6

MUST READS

6.1 Ways To Increase Your Chances Of Getting Hired

Looking for a job can be challenging, but not getting interview calls can be demotivating.

So, if you have been continuously applying for jobs haven't heard back from any company, here are some of the possible reasons you should know:

- **Resume issues**
  - ➯ Your resume isn't tailored to the job - Customize your resume to match the job requirements and show relevant experience and skills.
  - ➯ Your resume isn't formatted correctly for an ATS - Make sure to include relevant keywords with clean and simple formatting to be read correctly by ATS.
  - ➯ Grammar errors in your resume - Before submitting, always proofread your resume to avoid any grammatical or spelling errors.
- **Skills and Qualifications**
  - ➯ Lack of relevant skills and experience - Check the job role to understand the relevant skills or qualifications required.

- Lack of industry knowledge and technical skill - Research the industry and job requirements to make sure you're on top of the latest trends and technology.
- Inadequate collaboration skills - Show how you worked well with others to achieve your goals.

If you are continuously getting rejected or not hearing back from employers, it's important to take a step back and evaluate your approach. This introspective process will help you identify potential problems with your way of handling interviews and find solutions to improve your chances of success. If it has been a long time since you have given interviews and have not heard back even after you feel like everything went well, here are some of the possible reasons you should know:

- **Interview Performance**
  - Unprepared interview answers - Prepare the common interview questions and practice responses beforehand. For this, mock interviews always work best.
  - Poor body language - Pay attention to your body language, eye contact, and tone of voice to show confidence and enthusiasm.
  - Lack of enthusiasm for the role - Show your passion and interest in the job by researching and asking thoughtful questions.

- **Other factors**

Poor communication skills -	Practice active listening and articulate your ideas to improve your communication skills.
You are way too negative -	Maintain a positive outlook and focus on opportunities that are available to you.
Not following up -	Always follow up with a thank-you note or email after the interview to reiterate your interest in the job.
Asking irrelevant questions at the end -	Make sure your interview questions are relevant to the job and show interest in the company and role.

Understand that the job search is a two-way street. You need to find the right match for both you and the company.

6.2 The Most Effective Way to Boost Your Interview Skills

When it comes to job interviews, feeling nervous is quite common among candidates, regardless of their level of experience.

However, one factor that will help you stand out is your level of familiarity with the interview process. The more you do something, the more comfortable and familiar it becomes.

This is where practicing comes in.

Practice makes perfect, and the more you practice, the more confident you will become in handling the interview situation. This can also help you identify areas you need to work on, such as speaking clearly, answering questions with precision, and presenting yourself professionally.

One highly effective way to prepare for an interview is by taking mock interviews.

A mock interview is a practice interview that simulates the real interview experience. You can do this with a friend or family member, or even a professional coach or mentor.

- **Here are the top benefits you can experience from taking mock interviews:**
  - ➯ Receive feedback on every answer
  - ➯ Learn do's and don'ts of job interview etiquette
  - ➯ Reduce interview stress
  - ➯ Identify knowledge gaps
  - ➯ Practice your communication skills
  - ➯ Develop better time management skills
  - ➯ Practice your negotiation skills
  - ➯ Improve confidence

Mock interviews can boost your interview skills by giving you the edge you need to stand out from the competition. So take time to practice and prepare, and you'll be ready for a successful job interview.

6.3 Phrases to Sound More Confident in an Interview

In a job interview, it's evident that the way you present yourself can make or break your chances of landing the job. Every word you speak is evaluated, and the phrases you use can significantly impact the interviewer's perception of you.

Therefore, here's a list of a few confidence-boosting phrases you can use in an interview to sound more professional and self-assured.

- **When the interview starts, it's crucial to make a positive impression. You can use these phrases to get started on the right foot:**
  - "Thank you for taking the time to schedule a meet with me."
  - "I really appreciate being considered for this role."
  - "I was so excited when _____ told me about this position."
- **During the interview, you'll want to convey that you're the right candidate for the job. Use these phrases to explain how you'll add value, mention your long-term plans with the company, and show that you're a team player:**
  - "In my past roles, I have done [action] and achieved [results] within [timeframe]."
  - "The job role perfectly aligns with my long-term goals, and I'm very excited to continue to build my career here."

  - "One of my strengths is being able to work with others in a way that is effective and efficient."

- **End the interview on a good note by using these phrases:**
  - "The position sounds like the right fit. I am excited about the next step, so please do let me know if you need anything else from me."
  - "Can you please tell me more about the goals that you are trying to meet this quarter?"
  - "Thank you again for taking the time to talk today. Have a great day."

By using the right phrases, you can demonstrate your confidence and competence, make a lasting impression, and increase your chances of getting the job.

6.4 What Should You Do When You Don't Know The Answer In An Interview?

The thought of being unable to answer an interview question is scary for many candidates. Sometimes you don't know the answer or become nervous or unsure of the topic.

It's completely fine if you face this situation. Understand that even HR doesn't expect you to answer all the questions perfectly.

So, what's important is knowing how to respond when you don't know the answer. This will make you stand out from the crowd and help you make the most of such a situation.

I'm sharing 5 sample responses you can use in this situation:

Option 1 (Shows that you are motivated)

Thank you for asking this question. However, I need to become more acquainted with this subject. But I will definitely do some research on this.

Option 2 (Shows that you are a fast learner)

I won't be able to provide you with an exact answer right now. But I am a fast learner and will quickly learn under your mentorship.

Option 3 (Best for technical questions)

I can't find an exact answer. Please allow me some time, and we can return to this later.

Option 4 (If you don't understand the question)

I needed help understanding the question correctly. Could you please simplify and rephrase it. I don't want to misinterpret the question.

Option 5 (Redirect the conversation to the topic you are confident about)

While I don't have much experience in X skills, I have proper knowledge of Y. If the job requires me to learn X skills, I will be excited to expand my knowledge.

Additional points to help you handle this situation in the best way possible:

Practice this situation during the mock interview.

In your mock interview, consider including this situation so you can manage it more confidently.

Be honest

Be honest about your level of knowledge. Interviewers appreciate those who are willing to admit their limitations.

Stay confident while responding.

Maintaining a calm and confident posture even when you don't know the answer shows the interviewer that you can handle pressure and think on your feet.

Remember, one question or mistake doesn't stop you from being a good candidate for the job.

6.5 Right Way To Follow-Up After Your Interview

One of the most common misconceptions that candidates have is that they can sit back and relax after the interview. While this may be true in some cases, it is not a good idea to leave everything to chance.

Following up after the interview is an essential step, as it showcases your enthusiasm, keeps you in notice of the employer and increases your chances of getting selected for the job.

Here are 3 follow-up emails you should send after the job interview:

- **Thank you email**

  ↳ Goal: To thank the interviewer for the opportunity and their time.

  ↳ When to send: Send this between 24-48 hours after the interview.

Sample

"Dear [Interviewer Name],

I wanted to thank you for taking the time to speak with me about the [position] at [Company]. I enjoyed our conversation and I am grateful that I got the opportunity to learn more about the role and the company.

I am really interested in this position and I look forward to hearing back from you about the next steps."

Tip: Add a personal touch to your thank-you email by mentioning something you and your interviewer bonded over during the conversation.

- **Status check email**

  ↳ Goal: To check the progress of the hiring process.

  ↳ When to send: After 7-10 days of sending a thank-you email.

Sample

"Dear [Interviewer Name],

I'm checking to see if you have any updates on my application for the [position].

During our conversation on [day, date], you stated that the next step would be a call with a senior HR manager. I'd love to continue the conversation and take things ahead."

- **Further information email (Scenario 1)**
  - ➯ Goal: To provide additional information or ask relevant questions for the next step.
  - ➯ When to send: Send it in the next 24 hours after you receive the reply.

Sample

"Dear [Interviewer Name],

Thank you for responding and considering me for the [Job Title] position at [Company Name]. I am excited to take things ahead in the hiring process.

Before we continue, I have a few questions. [List your questions in a clean and simple manner]

Thank you again for your time and consideration."

- **Stay in touch email (Scenario 2)**
  - ➯ Goal: To maintain a relationship for future communication.
  - ➯ When to send: Send after receiving a rejection.

Sample

"Dear [Interviewer Name],

It was a pleasure speaking with you during the interview process for the [position]. I enjoyed our conversation and I am grateful for the opportunity to interact with you and learn more about the company.

I would like to thank you for letting me know your decision and I would like to stay in touch in future."

Follow-up emails can help you get your dream job. It shows that you are proactive and willing to take initiative.

6.6 Interview Etiquettes That You Should Follow To Ace Your Interview

Now that you've researched about the company and prepared your interview answers, it's time to focus on interview etiquettes.

Making a great first impression is essential for landing the job. Here are some basic interview etiquettes that you should observe to ace your interview:

- **Be punctual**
  - Arriving late for an interview can leave a negative impression on the interviewer. Always aim to arrive at least 10–15 minutes before the scheduled time.
  - Being on time shows that you are organized and can manage your schedule effectively.

- **Dress professionally**
  - ➾ Your appearance plays a crucial role in making a good first impression on employers.
  - ➾ Dress professionally and appropriately for the interview, and make sure to keep your hair and face groomed. How well you can take care of yourself is a direct indicator of how well you can take care of your responsibilities and tasks.
- **Listen carefully**
  - ➾ Pay careful attention to the questions being asked and respond thoughtfully.
  - ➾ Avoid interrupting the interviewer. Take a moment to organize your thoughts, and then answer.
- **Positive body language**
  - ➾ Maintain good body language during the interview. Sit up straight, avoid fidgeting, and look the interviewer in the eye.
  - ➾ These gestures show confidence, engagement, and professionalism.
- **Send a Thank you note**

After the interview, send a thank-you note to the interviewer.

Sending a "thank you" email can help the applicant stand out from the other candidates and demonstrate his professionalism, enthusiasm, and communication skills.

This is what you can write in that email -

Dear [Interviewer Name],

I wanted to thank you for taking the time to speak with me yesterday about the [Position] at [Company]. I enjoyed our conversation, and I am grateful for the opportunity to learn more about the role and the company.

I am really interested in this position and I look forward to hearing back from you about the next steps.

Again, thank you for your time and consideration.

Sincerely,
[Your Name]
Phone Number: xxxxxxxx

6.7 Body Language Tips To Show Confidence

Your non-verbal communication can significantly impact the impression that you make on your interviewer. It includes:

- How you carry yourself
- Your facial expression
- Hand gestures
- Tone of voice
- Eye contact etc.

Your body language conveys a lot about your confidence and psychology.

Here are some body language tips to remember when you go for an interview:

- **Make eye contact:** Maintaining an eye contact with the interviewer is extremely important as it shows confidence and respect.

Looking here and there while communicating indicates lack of confidence. It also indicates nervousness. Maintaining eye contact while speaking would engage the interviewer in the conversation.

However, it's important to understand that there is a difference between maintaining eye contact and staring. You should not look shocked or surprised while making eye contact.

Maintaining eye contact is a subtle art of creating an engagement.

- **Be responsive:** Always be responsive during an interview. If you don't know the answer, it's okay to let the interviewer know that you are not aware of that particular topic and you are interested in knowing more about it. It is important to create an impression on the interviewer that you have a desire for learning and up-skilling.
- **Body posture:** Slouching indicates disinterest or a lack of confidence. So, maintain a proper body posture during the interview and keep your shoulders straight. This shows that you are attentive, engaged, and interested. However, at the same time it is important that you look relaxed in a positive

way. The interview should be like a conversation between you and the interviewer and not like an interrogation.

- **Smile:** Maintaining a genuine and gentle smile can create a big difference and come across as an icebreaker. Make sure not to force a smile or grin unnaturally.
- **Avoid fidgeting:** Don't fidget during the interview. Try to stay still and focused. Continuously moving your hands, body and feet would indicate that you are nervous or bored. So, it's essential to stay calm and not make unnecessary movements which could be distracting.

With practice, you can use your body language to make a good impression and increase your chances of success in the interview.

6.8 A guide to reading job descriptions correctly

While searching for a job, you invest a lot of time looking for openings, revising resumes, submitting applications, and getting ready for interviews. But, to make sure that your search is as productive and successful as possible, it's important to read every single job posting in the right way.

- **By thoroughly checking the job description, you'll find:**

  ↳ key topics that the employer might address during the interview

- Important keywords that you can incorporate into your resume
- What is an employer looking for in an ideal candidate
- A clear understanding of the role
- Company's value and culture
- Potential red flags (if any)

Now that you understand the importance of reading the job description, there are certain elements to look out for that can help you quickly understand if a job description is right for you.

These are:

- Salary and benefits
- Contact info or link to apply
- Qualification and experience level
- Location and working arrangements
- Career growth and advancement opportunities
- Repetition of phrases of skills and responsibilities

Lastly, after reading the job description carefully, be sure about:

- Do I have these skills?
- Would I be happy with these responsibilities?
- Does this job align with my values and career goals?

By carefully examining these elements in a job description, you can make more informed decisions about the position to which you are applying.

6.9 13 Possible reasons you're not getting hired

Looking for a job can be challenging, but not getting interview calls can be demotivating.

If you are continuously getting rejected or not hearing back from employers, it's important to take a step back and evaluate your approach

So, here are some of the possible reasons you should know:

Resume issues

- Your resume isn't tailored to the job - Customize your resume to match the job requirements and show relevant experience and skills.
- Your resume isn't formatted correctly for an ATS - Make sure to include relevant keywords with clean and simple formatting to be read correctly by ATS.
- Grammar errors in your resume - Before submitting, always proofread your resume to avoid any grammatical or spelling errors.

Skills and Qualifications

- Lack of relevant skills and experience - Check the job role to understand the relevant skills or qualifications required.
- Lack of industry knowledge and technical skill - Research the industry and job requirements to

make sure you're on top of the latest trends and technology.

- Inadequate collaboration skills - Show how you worked well with others to achieve your goals.

Interview Performance

- Unprepared interview answers - Prepare the common interview questions and practice responses beforehand. For this, mock interviews always work best.
- Poor body language - Pay attention to your body language, eye contact, and tone of voice to show confidence and enthusiasm.
- Lack of enthusiasm for the role - Show your passion and interest in the job by researching and asking thoughtful questions.

Other factors

Poor communication skills -	Practice active listening and articulate your ideas to improve your communication skills.
You are way too negative -	Maintain a positive outlook and focus on opportunities that are available to you.
Not following up -	Always follow up with a thank-you note or email after the interview to reiterate your interest in the job.

Asking irrelevant questions at the end -	Make sure your interview questions are relevant to the job and show interest in the company and role.

Understand that the job search is a two-way street. You need to find the right match for both you and the company.

6.10 3 Salary Negotiation Tips I Teach My Candidates

(Triple your impact with this)

1. Research Thoroughly

Know the Market & Your Value: Use sites like Glassdoor to understand salary ranges and evaluate how your skills and experience align.

Sample Answer:

"Based on my research, professionals in this role within our region typically earn between X and Y, considering their contributions and market demand. Given my extensive experience and proven track record in Z, I believe a competitive offer would be on the higher end of this range."

2. Highlight Your Achievements

Quantify Success & Communicate Impact: Prepare to discuss specific, measurable outcomes from your past work.

Sample Answer:

"In my previous role, I led a project that resulted in a 20% increase in sales within six months, directly attributable to the marketing strategies I implemented. This achievement demonstrates my capability to significantly contribute to your team's targets."

3. Consider the Whole Package

Beyond Salary: Be open to negotiating benefits and other compensation if the salary is fixed.

Sample Answer:

"While I understand the base salary might be set, I'm interested in discussing how we might enhance the total compensation package with additional professional development opportunities or flexible working arrangements to create a mutually beneficial agreement."

6.11 Guide to Researching a Company Before Your Interview

Preparing for an interview isn't just about rehearsing answers to common questions; it's also about understanding the company you might be joining.

This one step can set you apart as an informed and interested candidate.

Here's how you can effectively research a company before your interview:

1. Start with the company website

- Explore the 'About Us' page.
- Understand their products/services.
- Familiarize yourself with the executives.

2. Dive into recent news and articles

- Search for recent news articles about the company.
- Look for features or mentions in industry-specific news sources.

3. Analyze their social media presence

- Stay updated with their latest posts and company updates.
- Look at their tone and engagement on platforms like LinkedIn and Instagram.

4. Understand the company culture

- Websites like Glassdoor can give insights into the company culture.
- Employee posts or company event photos can give you a feel for the workplace.

5. Research their competitors

- Understand the company's position in the industry.
- Know what makes this company unique compared to others.

6. Prepare questions based on your research

- Ask about recent company developments, future plans, or specific products that interest you.

7. Use your network

- Lastly, if you know someone who works there, ask for their insights.

Doing thorough research on a company is important. It helps you prepare better answers and understand if the company fits with your career goals and values.

Remember, an interview is a two-way street, and the more you know, the better you can assess if it's the right fit for you.

Chapter 7

Summary

7.1 The Ultimate Interview Preparation checklist

BEFORE THE INTERVIEW		
1.	**Research the Company**	• Study the company's website, mission, vision, and values.
		• Review recent news, press releases, and achievements.
		• Understand the company's products, services, and target audience.
		• Familiarize yourself with their competitors and industry trends.
2.	**Understand the Job Description**	• Analyze the responsibilities and requirements of the role.
		• Highlight key skills, qualifications, and experience needed.
		• Match your skills and achievements to the job requirements.

3.	**Prepare Your Resume and Documents**	• Ensure your resume is tailored to the job. • Proofread for grammar and formatting errors. • Prepare additional documents like your cover letter, portfolio, or certificates. • Print extra copies of your resume (if the interview is in person).
4.	**Prepare for Common Interview Questions**	• Practice answers to: ↬ "Tell me about yourself." ↬ "What are your strengths and weaknesses?" ↬ "Why do you want to work here?" ↬ "Where do you see yourself in 5 years?" ↬ Behavioral questions using the STAR method (Situation, Task, Action, Result).
		• Research role-specific and technical questions.
5.	**Prepare Questions for the Interviewer**	• Ask about team dynamics, growth opportunities, or company culture.
		• Avoid questions about salary or benefits in the initial stages.

6.	**Polish Your Communi-cation Skills**	• Practice speaking clearly and concisely. • Work on active listening. • Focus on maintaining a positive and professional tone.

The Ultimate Interview Preparation checklist

ON INTERVIEW DAY		
1.	**Dress for Success**	• Choose attire that aligns with the company culture (formal or smart casual).
		• Ensure your outfit is clean, ironed, and professional.
2.	**Organize Your Materials**	• Bring: ➩ Resume copies ➩ A notebook and pen ➩ Any required documents (ID, certifications, etc.) ➩ A list of references
		• For virtual interviews, keep digital copies ready.
3.	**Plan Logistics**	• Double check the interview date, time, and location (or meeting link).
		• Plan your travel route and aim to arrive 15 minutes early.
		• For virtual interviews, log in 5-10 minutes ahead.

AT THE INTERVIEW		
1.	**First Impressions Matter**	• Greet the interviewer with a firm handshake and a smile.
		• Maintain confident body language and good posture.
2.	**Active Listening**	• Pay close attention to the interviewer's questions.
		• Avoid interrupting and respond thoughtfully.
3.	**Showcase Your Skills with Examples**	• Use the STAR method (Situation, Task, Action, Result) to structure your answers.
		• Highlight achievements relevant to the role.
4.	**Ask Insightful Questions**	• Demonstrate genuine interest by asking about team dynamics, company goals, or growth opportunities.
5.	**Maintain Profession-alism**	• Stay calm and composed, even if faced with challenging questions.
		• Avoid negative comments about past employers or colleagues.

Post-Interview Actions

- Send a thank-you email to the interviewer within 24 hours.
- Reflect on the interview to identify areas for improvement.
- Follow up politely if you haven't heard back within the stated time.

7.2 Interview Vocabulary with Their Meanings

1. Accomplishment

Meaning: A notable achievement or success, typically in a professional context.

2. Collaboration

Meaning: Working together with others to achieve a common goal.

3. Efficiency

Meaning: The ability to do something in the best possible manner with the least waste of time and resources.

4. Innovative

Meaning: Introducing new ideas or methods.

5. Proactive

Meaning: Taking initiative and control, anticipating issues before they arise.

6. Team-Oriented

Meaning: The ability to work well within a team environment.

7. Leadership

Meaning: The ability to guide, direct, or influence others in a professional setting.

8. Adaptability

Meaning: The ability to adjust to new conditions or challenges easily.

9. Deadline-Oriented

Meaning: The ability to work efficiently under time constraints.

10. Strategic Thinking

Meaning: The ability to plan effectively for the long-term and make decisions that align with the bigger picture.

11. Multitasking

Meaning: The ability to handle more than one task at the same time.

12. Result-Oriented

Meaning: Focused on achieving outcomes and success.

13. Attention to Detail

Meaning: The ability to notice small details and ensure accuracy in your work.

14. Analytical Skills

Meaning: The ability to analyze information, identify trends, and solve complex problems.

15. Conflict Resolution

Meaning: The ability to resolve disputes or disagreements in a peaceful manner.

16. Self-Motivated

Meaning: The ability to push oneself to take initiative and accomplish tasks without external prompts.

17. Interpersonal Skills

Meaning: The ability to communicate and interact effectively with others.

18. Work Ethic

Meaning: The principle that hard work is intrinsically virtuous or worthy of reward.

19. Customer-Centric

Meaning: Focusing on creating a positive experience for customers.

20. Resilience

Meaning: The ability to recover quickly from difficulties or setbacks.

21. Negotiation Skills

Meaning: The ability to discuss terms and come to an agreement that benefits all parties.

22. Project Management

Meaning: The ability to plan, organize, and manage resources to successfully complete a project.

23. Time Management

Meaning: The ability to use time effectively to meet deadlines and manage workloads.

24. Diversity & Inclusion

Meaning: The practice of creating a work environment that respects and values diverse perspectives and backgrounds.

25. Self-Improvement

Meaning: The act of constantly striving to improve one's skills and performance.

26. Client-Focused

Meaning: Keeping the client's needs and satisfaction as the primary goal in a business relationship.

27. Technical Expertise

Meaning: In-depth knowledge of a particular area of technology or specialized field.

28. Cultural Fit

Meaning: The degree to which a person's values and behavior align with the company's culture.

29. Initiative

Meaning: The ability to take action without being told or prompted.

30. Problem-Solving

Meaning: The ability to identify solutions for challenges or issues in the workplace.

7.3 Common Interview Sentences for Different Situations

1. When Asked About Strengths:

- "One of my key strengths is my ability to stay organized, even when juggling multiple projects."
- "I consider myself a quick learner and am always eager to take on new challenges."

2. When Asked About Weaknesses:

- "One area I've been working on is my tendency to be a perfectionist, which sometimes leads to overanalysing details."
- "I've been focusing on improving my public speaking skills to become more confident in presentations."

3. When Asked to Explain a Career Gap:

- "I took time off to pursue personal growth and focus on professional development, and now I'm ready to return to the workforce with a fresh perspective."
- "I used the time to care for a family member, and during that time, I also completed relevant online courses to keep my skills updated."

4. When Asked About Your Motivation:

- "I'm motivated by challenges and the opportunity to make an impact. I enjoy being part of a team that works toward a common goal."
- "I'm driven by opportunities for growth and the ability to contribute meaningfully to a company's success."

5. When Asked About Handling Stress:

- "I handle stress by staying organized and breaking down tasks into manageable steps. This helps me stay focused and efficient."
- "I prioritize open communication with my team and manager, which helps reduce unnecessary stress and ensures we're on the same page."

6. When Asked About Working in a Team:

- "I enjoy collaborating with others, and I believe diverse perspectives lead to the best solutions. I'm always willing to support my team members."
- "I find that teamwork brings out the best in me, and I always make an effort to ensure good communication and mutual respect within the team."

7. When Asked About Long-Term Goals:

- "In the long term, I aim to continue growing in this industry, eventually taking on more leadership responsibilities and making a strategic impact on the company."
- "I see myself developing my skills further and eventually stepping into a role where I can mentor others and contribute to the organization's long-term vision."

8. When Asked About Handling Conflict:

- "I handle conflict by addressing it calmly and professionally, focusing on finding a solution that works for all parties involved."

- "I believe in open communication and am willing to listen to all sides before finding a resolution that benefits everyone."

9. When Asked About Time Management:

- "I prioritize tasks by deadlines and importance. I also break down larger projects into smaller, manageable tasks to ensure everything gets done on time."
- "I use digital tools to help organize my schedule, which allows me to stay on track and meet deadlines efficiently."

10. When Asked About Leadership:

- "In my previous role, I led a team of five to successfully complete a project ahead of schedule. I believe in leading by example and supporting my team members to achieve their best."
- "I believe effective leadership is about understanding the strengths of each team member and leveraging those strengths to reach our common goals."

11. When Asked Why You Want to Join This Company:

- "I admire your company's commitment to innovation and its strong company culture. I'm excited about the opportunity to contribute to your ongoing success."
- "Your company's mission aligns with my professional values, and I believe my skills will allow me to make a significant contribution to your goals."

12. When Asked About Your Achievements:

- "In my previous role, I successfully managed a project that resulted in a 25% increase in efficiency. It was a challenging but rewarding experience."
- "I received recognition for my ability to meet and exceed sales targets, and I consistently maintained the highest customer satisfaction rates in my department."

13. When Asked About Handling Change:

- "I embrace change as an opportunity for growth. I've learned to adapt quickly and maintain focus on achieving the objectives despite new challenges."
- "I've successfully navigated several organizational changes in my previous roles by staying flexible and positive about the direction we were headed."

14.During Salary Negotiation

- "I've researched the market value for this position, and based on my experience and the skills I bring to the table, I believe a salary in the range of [state your expected salary range] would be a fair compensation."

15.When Handling a Lack of Experience in a Specific Skill

- "While I don't have direct experience with [specific skill], I'm eager to learn and have successfully developed similar skills in my previous roles. I'm confident that I can quickly adapt and apply this new skill effectively in the role."

Community Network

Instagram – 2M+ Followers

Follow for short, impactful videos that will help you **land your dream job!** Discover answers to **important interview questions,** actionable **career tips**, **mastering salary negotiations**, and expert advice on crafting a professional resume. Learn the best **job search strategies**, how to **stand out in interviews**, and the secrets to **landing your dream job**. Plus, learn how to **optimise your LinkedIn profile** to ensure recruiters notice you. Whether you're a fresher or an experienced professional, these tips will help you succeed in your career.

Scan here to follow and be part of the journey!

YouTube – 1.1M+ Subscribers

Subscribe for in-depth, well-researched content that dives deep into every aspect of landing your dream job. Explore comprehensive tutorials on answering **important interview questions**, mastering **salary negotiations,** and conducting **salary research** to ensure you're compensated fairly. Learn how to craft a **winning resume**, ace your **LinkedIn profile optimization**, and implement job **search strategies** that work. You'll also discover which **careers are in demand** and how to tap into them, including tech, data science, digital marketing, Cyber Security Analysts etc. and receive actionable advice on transitioning into these high-growth fields.

Scan here and subscribe to my YouTube Channel!

LinkedIn – 220K+ Followers

By following me on LinkedIn, you'll gain access to **insightful posts, valuable industry insights, and actionable career** advice. Engage with my posts, share your perspectives, and be part of meaningful conversations that can expand your network. Building connections with the right people and networking strategically can open doors to new opportunities.

Scan here to connect and grow professionally!

Download "Diksha Arora" App

Now, take your interview preparation to the next level with "**Diksha Arora**" App, available on both **IOS** and **Android**.

Here's how the app can help you:

- **Sign Up for My Courses:** Access all my premium courses right at your fingertips and start learning anytime, anywhere.
- **Exclusive Services:** In addition to courses, you can explore tailored services such as Resume building and LinkedIn profile optimization
- **Free Access to Blogs:** Stay up-to-date with career advice and tips through my exclusive blogs, completely free when you sign up on the app.
- **Live Workshop Updates:** Get updates on my live workshops and be the first to know about upcoming sessions.

The **Diksha Arora App** is your one-stop destination to land your dream job

IOS:

Android:

Testimonials

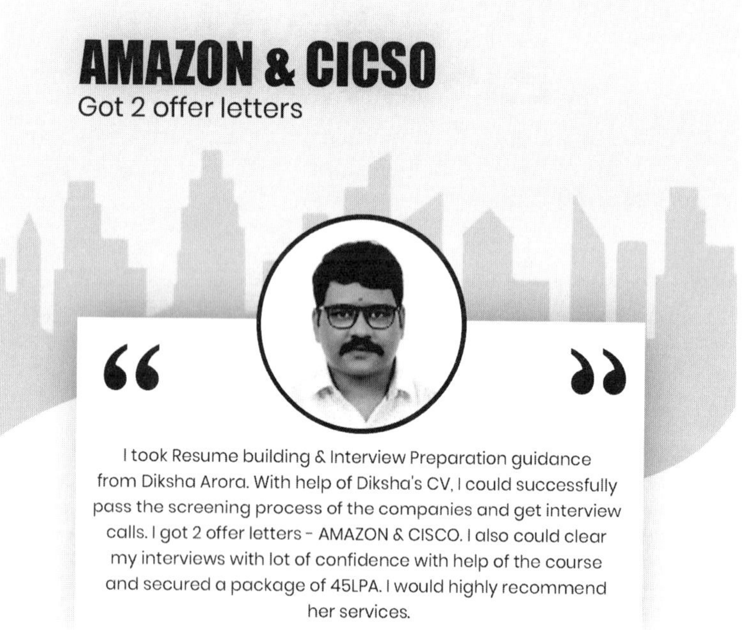

PLACED IN Deloitte

I got an offer letter from Deloitte.
I wish to extend my heartfelt gratitude for the invaluable support Diksha Ma'am provided in refining my resume, as well as for the enlightening telephonic guidance so graciously. It is with great pleasure that I inform you that I have received an offer letter from Deloitte, and I must say, her assistance played a pivotal role in this achievement. Her expertise and thoughtful advice were instrumental in navigating this process, and I am deeply appreciative of her time and effort. Thank you once again for your unwavering support. Anyone who is struggling to get a job, I would highly recommend her services.

AVIJEET BAL

PLACED IN Deloitte
Got 4 Offer letters
I got an offer letter from Deloitte and 3 more companies.
I am holding 4 offers as of now in this recessionary period.
All thanks to Diksha for helping me. Anyone who is struggling
to build a strong professional resume and clear their interviews,
I would highly recommend her services..
ANAND MAHAJAN

PLACED IN EuroAsia
BC Canada
I just cleared the interview and that too I don't have any
experience in the field I applied. I just changed the
industry from hospitality to accounting. I am starting
as an Accounts Clerk in Euro Asia one of the renowned
firm in BC Canada. Thank You Diksha.
ISHAAN SAHNI

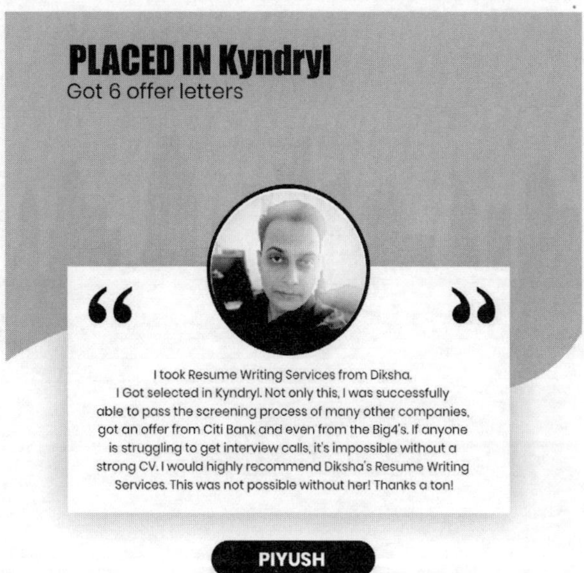
PLACED IN Kyndryl
Got 6 offer letters
I took Resume Writing Services from Diksha.
I Got selected in Kyndryl. Not only this, I was successfully able to pass the screening process of many other companies, got an offer from Citi Bank and even from the Big4's. If anyone is struggling to get interview calls, it's impossible without a strong CV. I would highly recommend Diksha's Resume Writing Services. This was not possible without her! Thanks a ton!
PIYUSH

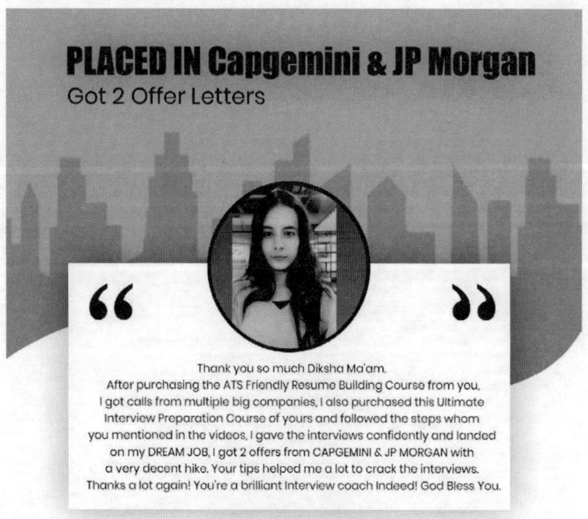
PLACED IN Capgemini & JP Morgan
Got 2 Offer Letters
Thank you so much Diksha Ma'am.
After purchasing the ATS Friendly Resume Building Course from you, I got calls from multiple big companies, I also purchased this Ultimate Interview Preparation Course of yours and followed the steps whom you mentioned in the videos, I gave the interviews confidently and landed on my DREAM JOB, I got 2 offers from CAPGEMINI & JP MORGAN with a very decent hike. Your tips helped me a lot to crack the interviews. Thanks a lot again! You're a brilliant Interview coach Indeed! God Bless You.
HARSHALI LALE

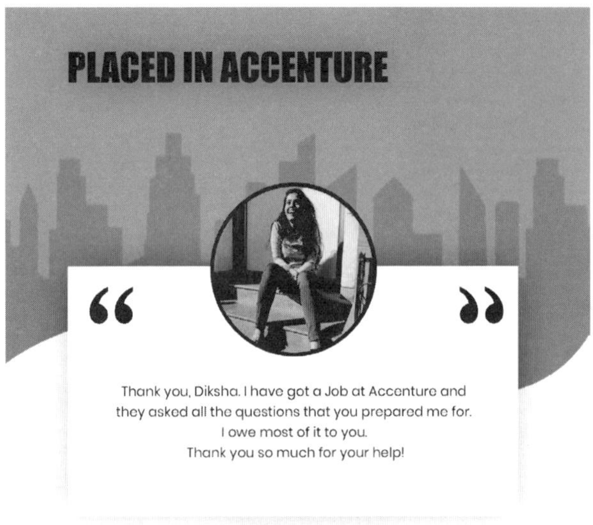
PLACED IN ACCENTURE
Thank you, Diksha. I have got a Job at Accenture and they asked all the questions that you prepared me for.
I owe most of it to you.
Thank you so much for your help!
KRUTIKA DIXIT

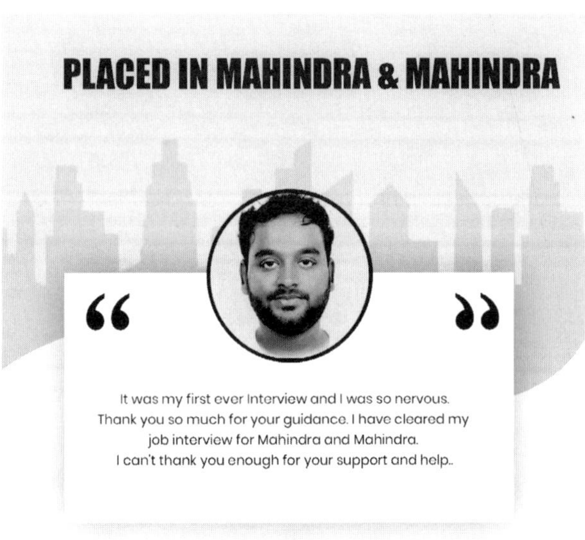
PLACED IN MAHINDRA & MAHINDRA
It was my first ever Interview and I was so nervous.
Thank you so much for your guidance. I have cleared my job interview for Mahindra and Mahindra.
I can't thank you enough for your support and help..
FAZAL SALMAN

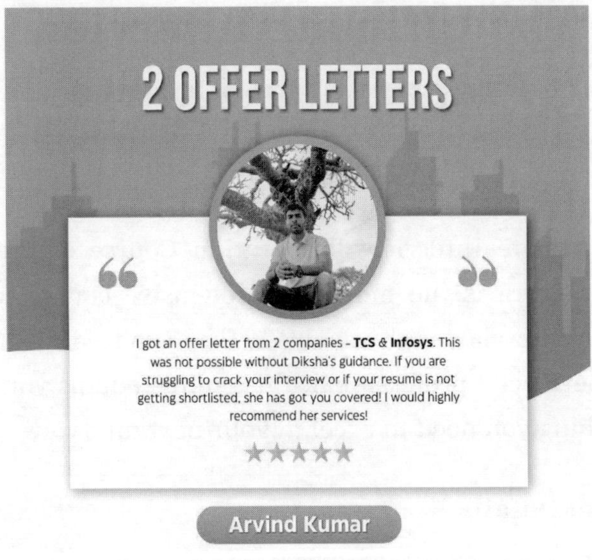
2 OFFER LETTERS
I got an offer letter from 2 companies - **TCS & Infosys**. This was not possible without Diksha's guidance. If you are struggling to crack your interview or if your resume is not getting shortlisted, she has got you covered! I would highly recommend her services!
Arvind Kumar

PLACED IN CAPGEMINI
With 100% Hike
I got placed in **Capgemini** as **Data Privacy Consultant** with **100% hike**. Thank you Diksha Mam for your mentorship and guidance. I would definitely recommend her interview preparation and resume building services to all the job seekers!
Akhil

The Ultimate Interview Preparation Course

The Ultimate Interview Preparation Course curated by Diksha Arora is the most comprehensive course to ace any job interview with ease. Whether you're a fresher or an experienced professional, this course equips you with everything you need to excel in your next interview.

Course Details

- **In-depth Modules:** Master common interview questions, advanced techniques, and strategies to handle the toughest interview situations.
- **Real-Life Scenarios:** Walk through sample answers tailored to a variety of job roles, so you'll know exactly what to say and how to say it.
- **Interview Mastery:** Not only will you learn the answers, but also the communication skills to impress potential employers and communicate effectively.
- **Professional Tips**: Gain valuable insights on salary negotiations and proven techniques to ace any interview. Learn to manage stress, tackle difficult questions, and present yourself with confidence in an interview.

- **200+ Sample Answers:** Access over 200 sample answers that will fit any job role.

Validity: Lifetime Access

Special Offer: Use the coupon code **JUSTFORU10** for a 10% discount on **"The Ultimate Interview Preparation Course"**. Don't miss out on this exclusive opportunity to invest in your future!

Scan here to enrol now ↓